OxB

MADAME TUSSAUD

List of books by the same Author

MADAME TUSSAUD

LEONARD COTTRELL
CADET EDITION

EVANS BROTHERS LIMITED, LONDON

Published by
EVANS BROTHERS LIMITED
Montague House, Russell square, London W.C.1

Set in 11 on 12 pt. Intertype Plantin and printed in Great Britain by
Cox & Wyman Ltd, London, Fakenham, and Reading

7/5532   PR2850

CONTENTS

ILLUSTRATIONS

INTRODUCTION

More than a century ago there died at her home in Baker Street, London, an old lady of eighty-nine. When she was a girl in France, King Louis XVI and Queen Marie-Antoinette ruled over their dazzling Court at Versailles. When she died, Queen Victoria had already reigned thirteen years. Born into a world of powdered wigs and aristocratic elegance, she died in a world of railways, top-hats and middle-class propriety. She lived through the French Revolution, knew most of its makers and many of its victims. She saw the rise and fall of Napoleon, and the restoration of the French monarchy, and she saw Great Britain grow into the world's greatest industrial and mercantile power. She not only knew most of the leading figures of her age, but through her art was able to preserve their likenesses for future generations. Her name was Madame Tussaud. This is her story, and that of the Exhibition of Waxworks which she founded.

To most British people the name Madame Tussaud is now as much a part of London as the Houses of Parliament, but few have more than the vaguest idea when and where she lived. I have talked to some who imagined she was still alive, still presiding in Marylebone Road, London, where, every year, hundreds of thousands see 'the famous and the infamous'. And in a sense she still lives. Her great-great-grandson, Bernard Tussaud, has inherited, through his father, grandfather, and great-grandfather the same uncanny skill in waxen portraiture which Marie Grosholtz as a young girl, learned from her uncle, Philippe Curtius, friend and companion of Mirabeau, Rousseau and Voltaire.

But art alone is not responsible for the continuing attraction

9

of the Exhibition. In my opinion, it survives and flourishes for two main reasons. The first is the British public's delight in a 'raree-show'. There is something in it of the travelling fair which delighted our country-bred ancestors in those far-off days before wireless and the cinema, when showmen in their lumbering caravans pitched on the village greens of England and Jack and Jill paid their pennies to see the Bearded Lady and the Siamese Twins. Madame Tussaud herself toured her Exhibition for years through the English shires and was a superb show-woman. Her flair for showmanship has passed to her descendants, though today it appears in a more streamlined form.

The second reason is the conservatism of the British public, which accepts and loves what is well-established and traditional. In no other country in the world is it possible for old music-hall artistes, long past their prime, still to delight audiences with songs and patter with which they triumphed a generation or even two generations ago. No matter if the jokes are mildewed and the voices cracked; the public loves them because they are institutions, part of the fabric of the national life. Not that there is anything aged and out of date in Madame Tussaud's, which uses every device of modern publicity and keeps resolutely abreast of the times. But, in a world which accepts as commonplaces the marvels of the cinema, of radio, television and pictorial journalism, surely only this affection for the traditional in entertainment can explain the continued popularity of the waxworks show.

Part of the story has, of course, been told before. Madame's own *Memoirs*, first published in 1838, remain practically the only source of material for her early life. Her great-grandson, the late Mr. John Theodore Tussaud, wrote a book called *The Romance of Madame Tussaud's*, shortly after the First World War, which added further chapters to the fascinating story. But since the publication of that book much interesting new material has come to light, in the form of letters, documents, early bills and Exhibition Catalogues which tell us much about Madame

10

Tussaud's later life after she brought her Exhibition to England. It is not always realized that for thirty years before settling in London Madame Tussaud and her two sons toured the rough nineteenth-century roads of England, Scotland, and Ireland, carrying her precious models in caravans, exhibiting in Town Halls, Assembly Rooms, inns and theatres; there were few towns of any size which she did not visit. She was also involved in the Bristol Riots of 1831, when her courage and coolness saved her models from destruction by the rioters. No doubt it was this experience, and the bitter memories it evoked of the French Revolution, which decided her to bring her Exhibition to London, where it has remained ever since.

Although this book deals mainly with the life of Madame Tussaud, it should be realized that she practised an art which existed for centuries before her time, an art whose origins are lost in the remote past. Before commencing her story, therefore, the reader might like to know something of the origins of wax-modelling itself.

Bee-keeping was practised by the oldest civilizations of which records have survived, and beeswax, as a modelling and preservative material, was thoroughly known by the ancient world. The Egyptians and the Babylonians used wax, particularly for embalming. The Egyptians, after removing the vital organs of their dead, often encased the viscera in wax before placing them in the four 'canopic jars' which accompanied the mummy in the tomb. Beeswax was also used freely in the embalming of the mummy itself, and in some specimens a wax plate has been found sealing the incision through which the organs were extracted.

The oldest form of sorcery known, the making of wax figures of an enemy, supposedly had its beginning with Egyptian, Babylonian and Indian magicians, from whom it spread to Greece and Rome. The Mayans of Central America also practised a similar form of black magic. Not only did they take revenge on their enemies, but they also claimed to be able to cure the sick by the use of magical wax figures. If a Mayan had a diseased arm, a sorcerer would be called in for consultation. He would then make a small wax figure representing the afflicted part, recite a spell over it, and burn or bury the effigy; the disease was believed to perish with the figure.

Another use of wax was in encaustic painting, in which the colour was prepared and ground in beeswax and cast in small cylinders, after which it was applied by means of a heated spatula. This may have been the method used for the decoration of the houses in Pompeii and Herculaneum. Pliny wrote of a special wax called *punica cera*, Punic wax, which was used by the Carthaginians. Wax tablets were also used by the Egyptians for writing, a custom which spread to Greece and Rome, where it persisted as late as the third and fourth centuries A.D.

But the most valuable use of wax was in the casting of metal objects by a system known throughout the world as the *cire perdue*—the 'lost wax' process. This system, discovered by the ancients and practised 3,000 years ago, is still in use today. With this method the artist first models in wax the head, figure or object which he wishes to cast in more durable material. If it is a small object, he first models it in wax in one piece; if larger, he makes it in sections. The wax being soft and plastic, great detail of design can be carved on its surface. Then the artist coats the surface with soft, wet clay which is allowed to harden. When sufficiently hard, the mould thus formed is heated and the melted wax pours out of a vent at the base. All that remains to be done is to fill the clay mould with molten metal, which sets. Then the mould is broken, revealing the completed cast. This was the method used by the sculptor who made the fine bronze dancing figure and other animal figurines from Mohenjo-daro in the third millennium B.C. It was also used by the Aztecs in America, and, of course, in Europe by classical, medieval and Renaissance sculptors and metal-workers. Michelangelo, Leonardo da Vinci and Benvenuto Cellini were all familiar with it.

Madame Tussaud and her many predecessors made their

wax figures by the reverse process; they first mode
heads in clay, surrounded the model with a clay mould
sections which could subsequently be removed, then b
sections of the mould together and filled the shell wit
wax, pouring away the surplus when the wax had fo.....u an
outer crust about one and a half inches thick.

Although sacred figures in wax have adorned European
churches for centuries, it is not known when the first lay exhibition was held, though they are known to have existed in the
sixteenth century. Not long ago Westminster Abbey reopened
its own collection of wax figures of royal personages, which were
carried at their funeral processions. The earliest is a rather
ghastly figure of Queen Elizabeth I, which was remade in 1760,
though the face may be original. Some of the effigies are re-
markably fine, particularly that of Charles II, perhaps the most
realistic portrait of him that exists.

But there was another channel along which the art of wax
modelling developed in the seventeenth and eighteenth centuries. In the days when the medical profession could not easily
obtain bodies for dissection, it was necessary to have some means
by which the structure of the human body, and the progress of
diseases, could be exhibited to students. The art of the wax
modeller was put to a practical use.

I have before me an advertisement by a certain Madame
Hoyo, one of Madame Tussaud's many rivals, in which one of
the figures is made to serve the purposes of both entertainment
and instruction. One of Madame Hoyo's groups represented
'A History of Samson at the time of being betrayed into the
hands of the Philistines, by Delilah. As an anatomical study,
the figure is worthy of the inspection of all Gentleman of the
Faculty, which after a thorough view of the Group is anatom-
ized in your presence, and accurately described—the head and
breast are opened, and the interior is exposed, with the animal
and vital parts, also the muscles, veins and arteries of the left
arm. It weighs 300 lb. of solid wax, cost 500 guineas, and took
the Artist two years to finish.'

Dr. Philippe Curtius, Madame Tussaud's uncle, who taught her the art, began his career as a modeller by making anatomical studies of this type, though he was already familiar with exhibitions of waxworks devised purely for entertainment. A hundred years before he was born, the Italians were acknowledged masters of the art, and in France, the country of his adoption, there had been exhibitions long before Curtius opened his 'Cabinet de Cire' in Paris.

Dr. Curtius himself modelled miniature figures in wax, and one of these, 'the Dying Philosopher', can still be seen in the Entrance Hall of the modern Exhibition in Marylebone Road.

There were many exhibitions of waxworks in eighteenth-century England. One of the most famous was that of Mrs. Salmon; there is a reference to her in the *London Journal* of James Boswell for 1763.

But it is time to leave the early history of waxworks and to introduce the reader to Madame Tussaud herself. The first part of the book describes her childhood and early life in Paris, where she modelled for her uncle, through whom she became directly involved in some of the most dramatic events of the French Revolution. The second part carries the story from her arrival in England in 1803 down to her death in 1850. The third and final part describes how the Exhibition has developed since her death, and how it has continued to reflect the pageant of British history, adapting itself continuously to the changing times, right down to the present day, when the popular heroes and heroines of the age, film, stage, radio, TV and sporting celebrities, take their place beside the kings and queens, statesmen and felons who drew the crowds in Madame's day.

In gathering the material for this book, I have been helped in a very pleasant task by the friendly co-operation of the Tussaud family and their staff, particularly the late Mr. Reginald Edds, who was an enthusiast for Madame Tussaud and a patient and indefatigable collector of 'Tussaudiana'.

I am also grateful to the British Broadcasting Corporation for allowing me to use some of the material broadcast in my radio programme, 'The Story of Madame Tussaud', and to Messrs. Hutchinson & Co. (Publishers) Limited, London, for permission to reprint extracts from John Theodore Tussaud's *The Romance of Madame Tussaud's.*

CHAPTER ONE

THE CURIOUS DR. CURTIUS

The first step leading to the founding of Madame Tussaud's Exhibition was taken by the Prince de Conti, cousin of Louis XV, when he walked into a house in Berne, Switzerland, in the year 1761. The house belonged to a Dr. Philippe Curtius, who had converted it into a small museum in which he exhibited miniature wax portraits of his friends and notable people of the neighbourhood.

The history of this medical modeller is curious, and his character more so. Born at Nockach, on the Rhine, in 1737, he was practising as a physician in Berne while still in his 'teens. He had an extraordinary skill in modelling, and to help him in his studies he used to make models of anatomical subjects in wax. Later, at the request of friends, he began making miniature wax portraits, and it was to an exhibition of these that the Prince de Conti paid a visit in 1761. His Highness was so impressed with these that he invited the Doctor to Paris, where, he assured him, such an exhibition would be bound to bring him into the favour of Parisian society. The Prince even offered to provide the Doctor with suitable studios in which to carry out his work. Curtius accepted the offer, and the Prince, true to his word, ordered apartments to be prepared at the Hotel d'Allegré, in the Rue St. Honoré. For the next few years Curtius was occupied, according to Madame Tussaud, 'in executing orders for his patron, whose liberality and kindness not only equalled, but rather surpassed, his promises'.

Curtius had a sister, Marie Grosholtz, the widow of a distinguished Swiss soldier, Joseph Grosholtz, who served as

aide-de-camp to General Wurmser during the Seven Years'
War. He was a brave and able officer, and during the war 'was
so mutilated with wounds that his forehead was laid bare, and
his lower jaw shot away, and supplied by a silver plate' (*The
Memoirs*). Both he and his wife were distinguished members of
Swiss society.

In 1761, two months after the death of her husband, Marie
Grosholtz, who was then living in Strasbourg, gave birth to a
daughter, also named Marie. For the first five years the little
girl lived with her widowed mother, mainly at Berne, and from
time to time Dr. Curtius paid fleeting visits to Berne from Paris.
His business was prospering, he was unmarried, and he frequently asked his sister to join him with her daughter. At last
she agreed, and in 1766 moved from Berne to Paris. From this
time onward young Marie Grosholtz was treated by her uncle as
his adopted daughter.

So began the most exciting and memorable period of Marie's
life, for during the next twenty years she was to be at the very
heart of the revolutionary storm. It was her fate to live with the
Court of Louis XVI and Marie-Antoinette during its final blaze
of splendour, to see that glittering world topple to its fall, to
see the monarchy overthrown, and to be forced to model the
heads of her former friends and patrons, often brought to her
uncle's studio still warm from the guillotine. Later she watched
some of the chief architects of the Terror, Danton, Robespierre,
Marat, themselves fall to the knife, and again she had to perform the same ghastly office. It was her fate because that
strange figure, her uncle, the doctor-modeller from Berne, became an intimate companion of many of the revolutionary
leaders.

Unfortunately, Marie Grosholtz has not left a diary, so that
we have to rely, for an account of this period of her life, on a
long-winded book of *Memoirs* published forty years after the
principal events had taken place; and written, not by Marie herself, but by a certain Francis Hervé, Esq., from material
which she supplied. Mr. Hervé, announced on the title page

as 'Author of *A Residence in Greece and Turkey*', has succeeded in enveloping Marie's story in clouds of pompous verbosity, liberally padded with his own moral reflections. Madame Tussaud is said to have been a brilliant and vivacious talker, and perhaps, like many good conversationalists, she disliked writing and was not very good at it. It is a pity that soundrecording was unknown in her day, so that we cannot hear her authentic voice, which speaks to us now only in Hervé's ponderous periods.

In 1766, when Marie Grosholtz and her mother arrived in Paris, the national pride of France was at a low ebb. At the Treaty of Paris, signed a few years earlier, Canada and North America had been ceded to England, there had been bitter losses in India, and the French Navy was shattered. Across the Channel, William Pitt had risen from his sick-bed to make his historic speech of sympathy with the American colonists, whose murmurings of 'No taxation without representation' found an echo in the minds of French liberal thinkers. Rousseau's *Contrat Social*, with its searching speculations into accepted religious and moral beliefs, had aroused such a storm that he had fled for a time to Scotland to take refuge with David Hume. The corrosive pen of the ageing Voltaire had never been more active, and the mind of France was in ferment.

Among the minds so stirred was that of Philippe Curtius, though whether from principle or self-interest it is difficult to judge. Certainly, from Marie's account of her childhood in Paris, it is clear that in the 'sixties and 'seventies he was socially intimate with some of the most liberal minds of his time: 'Early accustomed to sit at her uncle's table [writes Hervé] she was ever in the habit of hearing the conversation of adults, and persons of superior talent. Full well she remembers the literary discussions which were sometimes conducted with much bitterness by the opposing partisans of the favourite authors of the day.' Among these intellectuals she mentions in particular Jean Jacques Rousseau, Voltaire, Lafayette and Benjamin Franklin.

It is a pity that none of these conversations is described,

though, of course, it is unlikely that Marie, dictating her memories late in life, could have remembered much of what took place when she was a small child. Nevertheless, her recollections show that her observation must have been extremely keen and her precocity remarkable. Already we can detect the eye of the artist in her descriptions of the distinguished guests who argued around her uncle's table. There sits Voltaire 'very tall and thin, with a very small face, which had a shrivelled appearance and he wore a large flowing wig, like those which were the mode in the time of Louis the Fourteenth . . . dressed in a brown coat with gold lace at the button holes . . . a little cocked hat, large shoes . . . and generally striped silk stockings'. Near him sits Rousseau 'very much below the middle height, and inclined to be stout; he wore a short round wig with curls, something like that worn by George the Third . . . dressed in a snuff-coloured suit, very plain, and much resembling the present garb of the Quakers; but at one period of his life he adopted the Armenian costume, wearing a long robe, trimmed with fur, and a cap of the same material. Voltaire was ever gay, whilst Rousseau was generally the reverse, and rather misanthropic'.

Rousseau had every reason to be morose, as, according to Marie, his rival Voltaire was in the habit of mentally digesting Rousseau's ideas, which were freely expressed at her uncle's table, and later publishing them as his own. 'When Voltaire retired then would Rousseau give free vent to all his rage against his arch-rival, till he would exhaust all the abusive vocabulary of the French language in expressing his wrath, exclaiming "*Oh le vieux singe, le scelerat, le coquin!*" until he was fatigued with the fury of his own eloquence.'

The Marquis de Lafayette, later to become one of the leaders of the American colonists in their revolt against Britain, is also described: 'Elegant in his manners, full of vivacity . . . a tall, handsome young man, dressed in the costume then worn by a gentleman who affected not the extreme of fashion, nor the reverse . . . he was constantly with Franklin, and from him Lafayette imbibed those ideas which led him to cross the

Atlantic.' Dr. Franklin is described as 'a stout man, about five feet ten inches in height; his eyes grey, his complexion light. His personal appearance was that of the most perfect simplicity, his manners truly amicable'.

In vain we search Hervé's pages for a phrase which will give us a glimpse into the minds of these figures. They passed before us like Marie's waxworks . . . 'he was remarked for having particularly fine legs, his hair was very long and grey.'

There are, however, one or two occasions when the figures move. We see Mirabeau repeatedly getting drunk: 'He . . . was addicted to inebriety, so that, before he quitted the house, he became so disgusting that her uncle always declared he never would invite him again. Yet . . . such were the effects of his fascination, that he was sure to receive from M. Curtius another invitation, who, forgetting all that was disagreeable in the talented orator, was charmed by the engaging powers of his conversation. Although of noble birth, to display his contempt of rank and title, he took a shop, and sold cloth by the yard. He was a great libertine and spendthrift. Having dissipated a large fortune, he became overwhelmed with debts and embarrassment.'

From an early age Marie Grosholtz showed that she had inherited her uncle's gifts as a modeller. Perhaps he detected this even before she left Switzerland; it may have been one of the reasons why he invited her to come to Paris. Watching him at work in his studio, it is natural that the child should have tried to imitate her uncle. What is surprising is that she 'so closely imitated him that it was impossible to distinguish as to the degree of excellence between their performances'. At first she modelled fruit and flowers in wax, but soon she began portraiture, with such success that she was allowed to take casts from the heads of Voltaire, Rousseau, Franklin, Mirabeau and others. Some of these heads, said to have been modelled by Marie when a girl in her 'teens, still form part of the Exhibition today, and show that she possessed an amazingly precocious talent.

21

One of the most curious features of Madame Tussaud's memoirs is that, though they are full of pen-portraits of the distinguished men who came to her uncle's studio, they do not contain a single description of Curtius himself; nothing of his character, his virtues, his faults, not even an impression of his appearance. That he became a man of some power and influence is evident, and he made a substantial fortune. By 1770 his 'Cabinet de Cire' had become so famous that he moved his original exhibition to the Palais Royal and opened a second Museum on the Boulevard du Temple. He seems to have been a shrewd combination of showman, artist and business-man.

Yet it is difficult to see what attracted to him so many among the intellectuals and aristocracy of France. In an age of such artistic refinement, an age which produced painters like Chardin and Fragonard, sculptors such as Guillaume and Clodin, wax modelling, however adroit, would hardly have been more than a fashionable novelty. In any case there was nothing new in museums of wax models. Perhaps the most likely explanation is that Curtius appealed to the vanity of man; that he was cultivated for the same reason which gives power to the fashionable photographers and social 'columnists' of our own age—the lure of personal publicity.

Among the great figures of his time, artists, philosophers, noblemen, politicians, Dr. Curtius moves like a shadow. Few of them mention him except in a casual and not always flattering way. His own niece, whom, one would have thought, owed him most gratitude, makes no comment on his character. He began his career under the patronage of a nobleman. In the pre-Revolutionary period he enjoyed the favour of the Royal Family and his niece became the intimate companion of the King's sister. Yet when the Revolution comes he is on friendly terms with its leaders, first with the Girondists and later, when they fall, with the Jacobins. Finally, he dies obscurely—by poison—while on a mysterious mission on behalf of the Republican Government. Though the shadow is faint, it does suggest the outline of an intriguer and time-server.

Most contemporary or near-contemporary references, apart from the *Memoirs*, are to his Museum or Salon. There is one in the *Dictionnaire de Conversation* which is worth a quotation: 'Every year he renewed his two Exhibitions and each month he produced something new. The first Salon was given over to the representation of important people and artists. In the other were to be found villains and people who had made their name in the more shady walks of life.

'As he modelled the heads of all the distinguished people of the Court and the town he kept one copy of all the most beautiful heads by reason of their character and appearance and placed them on show in his Salon. He modelled kings, writers, beautiful women and thieves. Among his collection were . . . Frederick the Great and Voltaire, Catherine II and J. J. Rousseau, Hayder Ali and the aeronaut Blanchard, Franklin and Cagliostro . . . and the Royal Family sitting at a meal and Louis XVI beside his brother-in-law Joseph II.

'The barker at the door called out, "Come in, ladies and gentlemen! Come and see the banquet—exactly as it is at Versailles! It only costs two sous and you can go right up to and all round the figures."

'Curtius made a display of his patriotism from the start of the Revolution. . . . He offered for the public approval or execration the men of the hour or the whirl of fashion, victors and vanquished, and awarded them a place of honour or infamy according to the circumstances. He became a weathercock, like so many men who did not boast about it and who had found for themselves a way of making money. . . .'

CHAPTER TWO

MARIE GOES TO VERSAILLES

There is a portrait of Marie Grosholtz made in 1778, when she was seventeen. It shows a slim, attractive young girl dressed in a tight-waisted gown of some dark stuff, with a spreading skirt, sleeves of foaming white lace, and a lace *fichu* pinned at the breast with a spray of roses. There are roses in her hair, which is brown, spreading in gentle waves around a vivacious, intelligent face with large eyes, inquiring eyebrows, sharp nose and strong, pointed chin. It is both a delicate yet strong face, with something of the expression, though not the features, of Fanny Burney; the same sharp alertness, poise and dignity, and the same slight suggestion of primness. This was the Marie known to the Court at Versailles, who walked and talked with Louis XVI and Marie-Antoinette in their days of splendour, who was an intimate companion of the King's sister, and on one memorable occasion slapped the face of his younger brother, the future Louis XVIII.

In 1774, when Marie was thirteen, Louis XVI ascended the throne with Marie-Antoinette, lovely, imperious, self-willed and obstinate daughter of the Emperor of Austria. The Queen knew what she wanted and was determined to get it, and from soon after her accession it was she, and not the King, who wielded ultimate power. Louis, intelligent and studious, went some way towards making the urgent reforms which his Ministers pressed upon him, but he was no match for Marie-Antoinette, whose extravagance he disapproved of, but did little to check. According to the *Memoirs*: '. . . His only attempts to repress the inordinate expenditure lavished in giving those sumptuous entertainments at Versailles, which roused the indignation of the people, consisted in satirical remarks, and sallies of wit, turning them into ridicule, in which he was very fertile, and ever displayed much talent in his reproving sarcasms; but the Queen, particularly skilled in repartee, repaid his philippic with interest; whilst, enchanted and blinded by the torrent of admiration which it ever excited, she had not the fortitude to forego those bright assemblies which drew so many satellites around her.'

Meanwhile, the King, with a shrug of his shoulders, would retire to his studies, or to his workroom where he made locks, an occupation to which he was so partial that, Marie says, 'he was engaged in [it] for some hours every day, and . . . many of those now on the doors of the palace of Versailles were made by him'.

It was this enchanting butterfly world, in which the bright courtiers and their ladies circled the Queen as the planets the sun, that Marie entered in 1780, when she was nineteen. Among the members of the Royal Family who patronized Dr. Curtius at his Museum in the Boulevard du Temple was the King's sister, Madame Elizabeth. She was a mild, pious young woman with a weak, gentle face. She greatly admired Curtius's work, and that of his niece, and one day asked if she could be taught the art of wax-modelling herself. Marie was appointed to teach her, and the two women became so attached to each other that eventually Madame Elizabeth asked the Doctor if he would permit his niece to live with her as her companion in the palace of Versailles. Curtius agreed.

It is difficult to form, from the *Memoirs*, an adequate estimate of Madame Elizabeth's character, as, like most of the members of the Royal circle, she has been heavily daubed with Hervé's whitewash brush. 'Strictly religious, and charitable, in the purest sense of the word . . . benevolent . . . generous . . .' are words which occur frequently; but it seems that the friendship between the Royal lady and her young companion was a sincere one, since Hervé, writing in 1838, can say 'so amiable does

Madame Tussaud represent her to have been, that even at this distant period she cannot speak of her without shedding tears. . . .'

Rising at six, the Princess would ride for an hour or two in the Park, then, after breakfast, she and Marie would spend the morning 'tambour-working', a form of embroidery originating in China, in which the fabric is stretched across a small circular frame called a 'tambour'. Reading, writing and playing the harpsichord were other occupations, and, of course, wax-modelling. The Princess was fond of making religious statuettes to present to her friends, but Marie mentions another occupation which throws a vivid light on the beliefs of the time. 'Madame Elizabeth [she says] would often model in wax the legs and arms of decrepit persons, who desired it, which were afterwards suspended at the churches of St Génevieve, St. Sulpice, and des Capucins du Murche des Enfans Rouge.' This is still practised in some of the country districts of France.

It is doubtful if Marie entirely shared the pious zeal of her benefactor. Much later in life she used to warn her sons to 'beware the three black crows, the lawyer, the doctor and the priest', and though in her declining years a friend persuaded her to devote more of her time to religious devotions, the same friend was horrified on finding, one day, that the Crucifix which she had presented to Marie was being used by her as a hatstand. But that was in later years, when life had hardened and embittered her.

Life at Versailles was not all pious works and religious observance. The early part of Madame Tussaud's *Memoirs* is full of descriptions of magnificent assemblies, of Court balls and fêtes at which the nobility of France danced, flirted, gambled, intrigued, and paid homage to their radiant Queen. Meanwhile, the State had a national debt of over 5,000 million livres, and the mass of the French people paid over half their income in taxes, much of which went to support this magnificence. In 1777 Louis, in an endeavour to straighten out the nation's finances, appointed Jacques Necker as Director-General of

Finances in succession to Turgot, the previous Controller-General. Turgot had made a gallant attempt to destroy the servitude of the peasants by a series of enactments designed to end the abuses under which they suffered. But those who had profited by these abuses, the nobles, courtiers, financiers, farmers of the revenue, supported by the Queen, conspired against him. The Queen urged his dismissal, and Louis, unable to resist her, gave way. Soon afterwards Turgot's enactments were repealed, and Necker, his successor, tried to find a way out of the difficulty by economy and raising foreign loans. For a time the threat of taxation on the incomes of the nobility was raised, and the Court was able to continue along the glittering and resplendent road which was to lead so many of its members to the guillotine. Meanwhile the Queen triumphed.

Madame Tussaud describes the magnificent theatre within the Palace, at which Italian operas and French plays were performed for the benefit of the Royal Family and the Court. If a foreign ambassador was present a play would be specially acted to pay him a distinguished compliment, and the actors, settings, and music were the finest that France could produce.

Gaming for high stakes was prevalent, the Queen, the Princess and other members of the Royal Family often losing large amounts. Marie recalls one occasion when the King paid a surprise visit to his sister's chambers when she was present. He asked to speak to the Princess, and seemed to imply in the tone of his voice that he wished the conversation to be private. But on Marie rising to withdraw, the King waved her back to her seat with the words, '*Restez, mademoiselle, restez.*' Then followed a conversation in a low voice in which the King was evidently asking his sister to oblige him in some request. But on the Princess refusing the King rose from his chair, turned on his heel and stalked out with the remark, '*Alors je suis tracassé de tous côtés*' (then I am worried on all sides). Marie suspected that it was an application for a loan, probably to pay a gambling debt.

Though he enlarges at great length on the formal pleasures

27

of Versailles, and makes occasional references to gaming, Marie's biographer says little of the love-affairs which must have been another of the principal amusements of the Court. But she told him one anecdote which probably gave her a secret pleasure. Marie, as her portrait reveals, was an attractive, almost a pretty girl, and her charms were paid the compliment of the attention of the King's brother, Monsieur de Provence, later to become Louis XVIII. The story is worth quoting in full, Hervéisms and all: 'Among the visitors to Madame Elizabeth, was often Louis XVIII, then called Monsieur de Provence; but as he carried his excess of *politesse* to a degree which savoured too much of gallantry to be consistent with his exalted character, according to Madame Tussaud's notion of things, he received from her a rebuke, which, although sixty years since, remains still forcibly impressed upon her memory. It so happened that his royal highness and she met on the staircase together, when he was disposed to carry his complimentary politeness to too practical an extreme, and she judged it high time to give him a slap on the face; which so covered the prince with confusion, that when questioned by Madame Elizabeth, on his entering her presence, as to the cause of his apparent embarrassment, his hesitation in replying at once displayed that he was not so perfect at subterfuge and repartee at that period, as he has since proved himself to be; and notwithstanding all his evasive answers, the princess afterwards discovered the cause of his discomfited appearance, and, for the future, his royal highness restricted his expressions of politeness and regard towards Marie within more moderate bounds.'

Louis XVI, who often talked with Marie, made a favourable impression on her. She comments on his ease of manner, his lack of hauteur and condescension which must have been common among many of the courtiers, and the comparative simplicity of his life. Her portrait of him, which still survives, together with those of Marie-Antoinette, and the two Royal children, suggests the affable, kindly and intelligent man whom she describes in her *Memoirs*. It is easy to see him, living quietly in the grandiose Palace of the 'Sun-King', intelligent enough to be concerned at the worsening state of his country, reading Voltaire and Rousseau, conferring with reformist statesmen, such as Turgot and Necker, but lacking the will to resist his captivating Queen, deriding her extravagances, but not checking them, allowing her, in the end, to dismiss his wisest counsellors and undo the reforms which might have averted the final catastrophe.

Banquet followed banquet, each more costly than the last, each trying to outdo its predecessors in rarity of food, richness of dress and splendour of entertainment. And then, into this dazzling scene walks the quiet, sober figure of Dr. Benjamin Franklin, now Minister of the newly recognized American Republic. Marie describes him as she saw him, a stout man with a wise, tranquil face and long grey hair, dressed in black, his clothes cut 'in the old style'.

Marie evidently liked Franklin. 'An agreeable companion,' she says, 'and his manners were truly amiable.' But as she danced with him, as in later life she liked to recall, she could hardly have realized that, calm and reasonable as he was, his ideas, and those of other gentle philosophers, were going to put out the bright lights of Versailles and send its gay occupants to ruin and death.

It is doubtful if she or many of the others who thronged its salons and widespreading gardens realized what was happening in the world outside the park gates. In the nine years in which she lived at Versailles, she told Hervé, it was remarkable how little notice was taken of the disturbances and political storms which were raging outside the palace walls. Sometimes, she remembered, she would find Madame Elizabeth weeping, particularly during the latter years of her stay, and 'could only suppose that her tears were caused by the increasing troubles which menaced her brother's kingdom. . . . But there appeared, generally, a sort of understanding, even amongst the attendants in the palace, that politics was a forbidden subject; so that it was only by accident that Madame Tussaud ever heard of the transactions which were occurring relative to the government, and threatening its dissolution, with that of the monarchy, and, in fact of all social order'.

Let us go for a moment outside those palace walls and see what was happening in France and the outer world. In 1775, five years before Marie entered Versailles, the resentment of the American colonists against British taxation, simmering for years, boiled over into open revolt. It was the year of Paul Revere's famous ride, of the signal light on the North Church, of the redcoats falling to the colonists' bullets at Concord, the beginning of the War of Independence. In the following year came the Declaration of Independence, and France, seeing in the American revolt a chance to avenge her humiliation over Canada, sided with the colonists. In 1777 Lafayette joined Washington, and in the following year the American Treaty was signed by which France formally came to the assistance of the Americans.

Meanwhile Franklin, who had helped to draw up the Declaration of Independence, had returned to Paris and was recognized as the Minister of the U.S.A. by France. When, in 1783, the American Peace Treaty was signed, the people of France could feel that, in helping to establish the independence of America, they had evened the score with Britain.

But intervention on the side of a republican revolt had led to the propagation of republican and revolutionary ideas. The influence of men such as Franklin and Lafayette was strong, as were the works of Rousseau, Montesquieu and Voltaire. Frenchmen began to look more and more towards the reform of abuses within their own country. Of these there were many. Tyrannical laws, unchanged since feudal times, held the peasants, who formed the majority of the population, in subjection to the nobility. There was the notorious *fief à mainmorte* by means of which a nobleman could claim the inheritance of all born on his estate, which was not repealed until 1788. There were the notorious *lettres de cachet* signed and sealed by the King and issued to the governors of prisons. The insertion of a person's name was all that was necessary to secure committal to the

Bastille. This kingly privilege was not abolished until 1789. But the deepest cause of anger was the appalling, hopeless poverty of the masses, especially the country people. France was then almost wholly an agricultural country and the bulk of the savage taxation fell on the peasant. In times of bad harvest, having yielded most of his produce to the tax-gatherer, he starved; yet the nobility, whose wealth was created by his labour, paid the lightest of taxes.

Now we return to the world which Marie Grosholtz knew. We enter through the park gates, past the great columned façade of the Palace, where lights glow within richly curtained rooms, to where the broad terraces descend to the lawns and woods beyond. It is a fine summer evening and a fête is in progress. Marie is describing it for us '. . . The gardens are illuminated, the waters playing; the variegated lamps are so introduced about the marble fountains that they appear as if mingled with the waters, communicating to their bright silver sheets all the resplendence of the prismatic colours which everywhere sparkle, as they reflect thousands of rays, which are emitted from innumerable lights, shedding their lustre in as many tints as the rainbow can describe. The most beautiful echoes also fill the air, produced by skilful musicians, who are judiciously placed in the numerous arbours, bowers, and grottoes, with which the gardens abound; the melodious tones from one horn are scarcely suffered to melt in air, before its fading note is heard from an opposite grove, gradually swelling into its round and fullest force, then gently dying away, until lost in the breeze, or hushed by the sound of falling waters, till again the ear will catch the more powerful notes of horns playing together in parts, and ending in a continued succession of the most harmonious strains. . . .'

So the nine years pass. The Queen glitters at her assemblies, the King talks to his Ministers, makes some concessions, then, at the will of the Queen, withdraws them with a sigh and goes off to his workroom to make locks. In another wing of the Palace the pious Madame Elizabeth models her waxen statuettes of saints, relieves her 'poor pensioners', or plays cards with her vivacious young companion. Then distant rumblings began to be heard outside the walls, faint and infrequent at first, then more insistent and often. Necker, whose reforms, like those of Turgot, offended the Court party, follows the latter into retirement. Calonne, favourite of the Queen, succeeds him, but on declaring an enormous deficit, has to flee the country. The aristocracy will not accept the least diminution of their power and privileges. Brienne succeeds Calonne, but does nothing. The King, more sensitive than most of his followers to the growing demands for reform, decides to make a gesture. In 1786 he had curtailed his expenditure and reduced his household, in order 'to be in a better condition to alleviate the distressed'. In 1788 he again reduces his household, and, on the demand of Parliament, still further diminishes his expenses. But with each new concession the public clamour grows until the King realizes that he will be forced to call the States-General, the ancient legislative assembly of France.

In times of political unrest there are minds which, like seismographs, are more sensitive than others to approaching shocks. Among these, not surprisingly, was Dr. Philippe Curtius. Early in 1789 he waited on Madame Elizabeth and explained that with regret he must ask that his niece be allowed to return with him to Paris. So, after a sad farewell to her royal mistress, Marie returned, after nine years, to live on the Boulevard du Temple. For her the magic horns of Versailles had sounded for the last time.

A corner of Madame Tussaud's atelier in Paris during the French Revolution. She is making, under duress, a death mask from the severed head of Marie-Antoinette

The Salon of Dr Curtius

CHAPTER THREE

REVOLUTION

On July 12th, 1789, a graceful, firm-featured woman of twenty-eight stood watching from the tall windows of her uncle's Salon, a shouting, gesticulating mob pouring down the Avenue du Temple and massing outside the gates of No. 20. Marie was not frightened, though her brown eyes were anxious as they turned from the animated faces of the crowd pressed against the railings to the calm, reflective figure of her uncle. If Dr. Curtius felt anxiety, he only betrayed it in the nervous jiggling of his eyeglass on its long silk cord. Occasionally a shout floated up from the hubbub:

'Give us the Duke of Orleans!'

'We want Necker!'

'Give us their figures, Curtius . . . and the King. *Give us the King!*'

There was a roar at this, and the Doctor smiled. Nothing, thought Marie, seemed to disturb him. Cold, self-contained, he was calmly deciding what to do, and having decided, nothing would deflect him from his decision. And almost certainly it would be the right one.

He had been right to take her away from Versailles. She could see that now, though at the time the sudden break with the Princess had puzzled and distressed her. But how could she have foreseen all that was to happen during the few months which had passed since she left Versailles? During the previous year, 1788, she had heard talk of the calling of the States-General. The historic Parliament of France, consisting of the three Estates—Nobility, Church and Commons—had not met

c   33

since 1614, 175 years ago. It was as if England in 1965 had decided to revive the Court of Star Chamber. There had been some concern about this at Versailles, but also much amusement at the trouble it had caused. The Court wits had found much diversion in the labours of the official archivists, who had to delve into piles of dusty documents to discover the ancient rules of procedure. Brienne, the Controller of Finance, had asked as many bodies as possible to help in collecting the documentation. Dossiers came in from all over the country. The office of Barentin, the Lord Privy Seal, was flooded with letters. One sheriff had written to say that although he could not find anything of value in his Record Office he was going to ask all the old men in his district for information.

All this had suited Brienne perfectly, for he had no desire that the States-General should meet soon, or that, when it did meet, it should be an effective legislative body. The decision to call it had been taken purely to meet the popular outcry. But after two months of muddle and confusion, Brienne had been replaced by Necker, the rich, incorruptible Genevan banker, who sincerely advocated financial reform—the same Necker whom Marie-Antoinette had contrived to have dismissed in 1781.

Under his leadership, the work of preparation went ahead more rapidly, though none too soon, for already there had been ugly incidents. On April 27th a paper manufacturer named Reveillon had been injudicious enough to complain that he was forced to pay his workmen 1s. 8d. a day, and that they lived less well on it than on their former wage of $7\frac{1}{2}d$. a day. Six hundred of them appeared on the streets, hanged the manufacturer in effigy, and, armed with clubs and torches, began looting. Troops were called out, the mob increased, and soon there was fighting in the streets, amid cries of 'To Hell with the nobles and clergy!' and cheers for the King, the Commons and Necker. Twenty people were killed and twice as many injured before the riot was quelled. In the country also there had been bread riots. Then on May 2nd the States-General had met, with the Third Estate (i.e. the Commons) in doubled numbers. Necker had wanted them to meet the King in Paris, but Louis refused, so the tradesmen, doctors and lawyers of the Third Estate, in their plain country clothes, crowded into the gilded Hall of Mirrors, where a bored but patient Louis listened to their humble addresses.

But when they met in formal session a few days later, their attitude was less humble. As the weeks passed it became clear that the Third Estate, which outnumbered the Church and Nobility, was determined on a redress of grievances. It demanded that the three Estates should meet as one Assembly, and not as three separate bodies. In June it adopted the title of the National Assembly. The King, supported by the nobles, ordered it to dissolve. It refused, and on June 20th members took the famous Oath of the Tennis Court, in which they swore to make a new Constitution for France.

Since that day, less than a month ago, Marie had seen appeals, conciliation and debate change to frustration, anger and the threat of violence. Events had moved from crisis to crisis. Necker had again been dismissed. The Duke of Orleans, another favourite of the people, had fallen under the Royal displeasure. Alarmed at the menacing attitude of the Parisians, the King had ordered troops to move towards the capital. Paris was full of foreign mercenaries, including the German soldiers of the Prince de Lambesc, hated equally by the people of Paris and the King's French troops.

Now it was the twelfth of July—a Sunday. Earlier that afternoon Parisian crowds were thronging the arcades of the Palais Royal—one of the few buildings which still survives from the Paris of Revolutionary times. It was a fashionable meeting-place, and among the crowd that afternoon was a young barrister, Camille Desmoulins. Young, irresponsible and eloquent, he had harangued the citizens on the dangers of the situation, referring bitterly to the dismissal of Necker and the Duke, and upbraiding the Parisians for their cowardice in the face of the King's troops. Passions were roused, someone shouted, '*Aux armes!*' a mob quickly gathered and one of their number suggested that they march to the Boulevard du Temple and demand from Curtius the busts of their favourites. It was this crowd which Marie watched as it seethed and murmured outside the gate, which the prudent Doctor had ordered to be shut. However, it was not, at this stage, a disorderly crowd. 'They were so very civil, and their general bearing so orderly,' says Marie, 'that I felt no alarm.'

Dr. Curtius handed over the busts of Necker and the Duke of Orleans, though when the demonstrators demanded that of the King he refused, observing that it was a full-length figure and 'would break easily'. To this, for some inexplicable reason, the crowd replied with 'Bravo, Curtius!' and then retired quite happily, carrying the busts on pedestals draped with crêpe, and shouting, 'Long live Necker! Long live the Duke!' and 'Down with the foreign troops!' Marie watched them go, then returned to her work.

It was not until some time had passed that she and her uncle were alarmed by the sound of distant shooting. Soon rumours began to reach them. The demonstrators had been fired on by some of the King's German mercenaries. The French Guards had come out on the side of the people. There had been a riot in the Tuileries Gardens. Finally, a few of the demonstrators, their clothes torn and bloodstained, returned to Curtius with a few fragments of the head of Necker, and the Doctor and his niece heard the whole story.

The demonstrators had paraded in an orderly manner along the Rue St. Honoré until, near the Place Vendôme, they met a detachment of German troops commanded by the Prince de Lambesc. These rushed upon the people, wounding several. In her *Memoirs* Marie stresses the fact that this brutal assault was made on a peaceful demonstration and that up to that moment there had been no provocation. But among the crowd was a private of the King's French Guard whose regiment had been in an affray with the Germans a few days earlier. Word quickly reached the French troops, who were in barracks close by, and they in turn rushed out and fired on the Prince's men, who retreated to the Gardens of the Tuileries.

These Gardens were a favourite haunt of Parisians and in that pleasant July afternoon men, women and children were enjoying their usual peaceful Sunday promenade. Suddenly the Prince de Lambesc's men burst into the gardens and charged on the people.

Throughout the night and the following day Marie heard the clanging of bells and the surge and tramp of mobs. The Champs de Mars was full of troops, and other detachments were said to be moving towards the city. The people raided the Hôtel de Ville, the Invalides, the arsenals, the gunsmiths—any place where they could get arms. Along the narrow, high-walled streets which straggled down to the Seine the excited crowds ebbed and flowed. Drums beat, men mustered and marched, and everywhere the cry was *'Aux armes!'* Meanwhile, the National Assembly sent representation to the King at Versailles, informing him of the state of excitement in Paris, and asking him to remove the troops which were the cause of so much apprehension. But Louis, a true Bourbon in his obstinacy, sent a cold reply. The King, he said, was the best judge of the necessity for the troops.

The fact that by Tuesday, the 14th, no further troops had entered Paris did not calm the fears of the citizens. The search for arms went on. The most urgent need was for powder, and this sent the patriots hurrying towards the Bastille, where large quantities were stored. For more than 700 years the grim, grey fortress, with its great drum towers, moats and drawbridges, had frowned down upon the district of St. Antoine—a dark symbol of the feudal age which had created it. Now its Governor, the Marquis de Launey, and 130 men were preparing its defences, and when the citizens saw the muzzles of guns pointing down at them from between the ancient battlements they sent a protest to the Municipality, whose deputies met the Governor and asked him not to fire on the people.

While negotiations were going on, an angry crowd gathered

in the outer court and threatened to attack. In vain the Municipality sent Thuriot, an elector, to summon the Governor to surrender. De Launey refused, and even as he carried the Governor's defiant answer back to the Hôtel de Ville Thuriot heard, from the direction of the Bastille, the crack of musket-fire and the swelling roar of the mob as they closed in to the assault.

Then came the deeper boom of cannon. Some of the French Guard and the Militia had brought up artillery and cannon-balls crashed into the heavy doors. The garrison set fire to hay-carts in a vain attempt to put down a smokescreen. Two citizens, at great risk, dragged them away. Another, Hulin, shot away the chains of the outer drawbridge which the defenders were trying to raise. The civilian mob, aided only by a few professional soldiers, stormed the heavily defended gateway with ferocious daring. Again and again they returned to the attack, though ninety-eight were killed and almost as many wounded. For two hours the cannonade thundered, then a paper was thrust through a crack in the gate, a threat by the Governor to blow up the Bastille unless the garrison was given honourable terms of capitulation. This only inspired the mob to sterner efforts. The guns opened again, and then, after a little time, the attackers saw through their smoke-blackened eyes a sight which set them cheering madly. Slowly the main drawbridge was coming down. It seemed impossible, the terrible old fortress, hated and apparently everlasting symbol of tyranny, was capitulating—after only a few hours—to a crowd of civilians! Wild with joy and relief, the mob stormed into the Bastille, and soon the bleeding heads of De Launey, the Governor, and Jacques de Fleselles, whom the mob believed had denied them arms, were being carried through the streets on pikes.

Below the towers were the dungeons, which Marie Grosholtz later saw and described to Hervé: 'They exhaled noxious vapours and stench and were infested by rats, lizards, toads and other loathsome reptiles. In an angle of each dungeon was a camp bedstead . . . of planks resting on bars of iron fixed to the wall. These cells were dark and hideous, without windows or apertures. . . . They were secured by double doors of three inches thick, the interior covered with iron places and fastened by strong bolts and heavy locks.' She also described the 'iron cages . . . eight feet high by six feet wide, formed of strong beams, strengthened further by iron bars. . . . An iron cage, about twelve tons in weight, was found with the skeleton of a man in it. . . .'

When the Bastille fell, there were still certain political prisoners in the dungeons, and these the crowd set at liberty. According to the *Memoirs*, there were sixteen, including 'an Irish gentleman named Clotworthy Skeffington Masareen, but he was not confined to the cells, but had an apartment on the first floor, and was merely imprisoned for his debts'. However, later research has reduced the number of prisoners to seven. One of them was the Comte de Lorge, who had lain in the Bastille for thirty years, and whose effigy can still be seen in the modern Exhibition in Marylebone Road. Marie made the original cast a few days after the fall of the Bastille, when the Comte was brought to Curtius's Salon so that she could model his features. Possibly the idea originated in the mind of Curtius or one of his friends—Robespierre, perhaps—of using the head in their propaganda campaign against aristocratic tyranny. Modelling it must have been a sombre task, though not so horrifying as those which Marie had to perform later; one wonders why Curtius entrusted the work to his niece, instead of doing it himself.

Later, in company with her uncle, she visted the Bastille at a time when it had become the show place of Paris. Citizens and their wives came in their thousands to see the dungeons, the iron cage and instruments of torture, and it may well have been this experience which impressed on Marie's practical brain the fascination which scenes and objects of horror exercise over the human mind. Certainly she made profitable use of this trait in later years. Her biographer, true to his nineteenth-century conception of female delicacy, always represents her as shrinking from the scenes of brutality and horror which she had to witness. She was, he says, 'prevailed upon' to accompany her uncle to the Bastille. She was 'impelled by anxiety' to watch the Queen going to execution, and so on. Yet was the real Marie so squeamish? After all, she belonged to the eighteenth century, a tough age, and all the impressions of her in later life suggest a woman of iron character. One cannot help feeling that the young Marie Grosholtz was made of harder material than Mr. Francis Hervé liked to admit.

During her visit to the Bastille she had an encounter with Robespierre; as with Monsieur de Provence, it was on the stairs. Whilst descending a narrow stairway in one of the towers, her foot slipped and she was saved from falling by Robespierre, who caught her in his arms with the words: 'It would be a pity for so young and pretty a patriot to break her neck in such a horrid place.'

She remembered this compliment fifty years later, which suggests that Marie had her usual share of feminine vanity. She had met Robespierre many times at her uncle's dinner-table and describes him at some length in the *Memoirs*: '. . . always extremely polite and attentive, never omitting those little acts of courtesy which are expected from a gentleman when sitting at table next to a lady. . . . His conversation was generally animated, sensible and agreeable; but his enunciation was not good . . . he had not the talent, energy or power of his auditors, which are so eminently conspicuous in Marat.'

She does not agree with contemporary apologists who represented Robespierre as incorruptible. She admits that at the height of his power he was living in a small lodging and dining on fifteenpence a day, but she also describes how Robespierre accepted from Dr. Curtius a bribe of 300 louis paid on behalf of a Monsieur Philipstal, a fellow-showman who exhibited a 'Phantasmagoria' in which he had inadvertently offended the authorities. We shall hear more of Monsieur Philipstal when we follow Marie to England.

When the novelty of viewing the Bastille was exhausted,

Parisians set to work to demolish it completely. Stones from the fortress were bought by patriotic citizens who built them into their doorsteps so that they might tread daily on the emblems of tyranny. A gentleman named Palloy contracted to demolish the building, and made a fortune exhibiting various relics in a museum which became one of the most popular shows in Paris. There were Bastille paper-weights, Bastille snuffboxes, Bastille inkpots—a torrent of bric-à-brac which filled the curio shops of Europe for years, and of which specimens can still be found. Later Marie acquired the key and other relics.

On the day following the fall of the Bastille, Louis entered the Parliament House at Versailles to inform the Deputies of the National Assembly that the troops would be removed. Although Bailly, one of the Deputies, had the courage to remind the King that the riots had been brought about by his own obstinacy, the Deputies as a whole cheered the announcement, and when the Queen appeared on the balcony of the Palace carrying the infant Dauphin, the emotional crowd was 'moved to tears'.

From the country came reports of widespread risings; there had been bread-riots, and in some districts châteaux had been burned. Then for a time order was restored in both the capital and the provinces. In Paris the National Guard, a citizen army, was formed to maintain order, and Lafayette became its commander, while Bailly, as Mayor of Paris, took charge of the civil administration. The King entered Paris in triumph as 'Louis XVI, the Father of the French, the King of a Free People', as an inscription over the Hôtel de Ville expressed it. Forty thousand of the City Militia, accompanied by citizens armed with pikes and clubs, lined his route, while great crowds shouted, 'Long live the Nation! Long live the King!' mixed with cries of 'Lafayette!' and 'Bailly!' At this stage the mass of the people were still prepared to believe that the King was indeed their champion, and that his actions concerning the troops and the dismissal of the people's favourites were due to evil counsellors. But the Queen and her friends remained under suspicion.

On August 27th, the National Assembly passed its Declaration of Rights and for a few weeks there was peace.

Then, early in October, came further outbreaks of rioting, the principal cause of which was a bread famine. There was an acute shortage of flour, and Necker was forced to buy abroad. In Paris menacing crowds began to gather and demonstrate. To add to the unrest news came that fresh troops had arrived at Versailles, and rumours were spread of a dinner at the Palace given by some of the Flemish officers at which the national cockade had been trampled underfoot. It was said that the Royal Family had been toasted, but not the nation. The people began to fear once again that the Court was planning to destroy their new-found liberties and reduce them to servitude. The distance of Versailles from Paris added to the anxiety. If only the King and the National Assembly were in Paris, where the citizens could keep an eye on them! The outcome was the famous march of the women on Versailles, 'wearing ribbons of all sorts, armed with sticks, pitchforks, pikes and muskets,' marching 'very clamorously, but in order and with determined step'—resolved to present their grievances to the King.

One can imagine the shock to Marie's Court-trained mind on hearing that the Royal apartments had been invaded, the Queen surprised, half-dressed, by a group of armed and angry women, and forced to fly to the arms of the King for protection; of the King's having to embrace one of these Amazons with a mollifying speech; and of that final, humiliating march to Paris —the Royal coach containing the King, Queen and the Royal children escorted back to the capital by a triumphant mob chanting, 'We are bringing the Baker, the Baker's Wife and the Baker's Errand Boy. . . .' And ahead marched two of the women each carrying on a pike the head of one of the Royal bodyguard.

So Louis became virtually a prisoner in the Palace of the Tuileries, which both he and the Queen hated. Paris hemmed them in. The Palace gardens were invaded on Sunday afternoons by the *bourgeoisie* and their wives. Louis missed his hunting. Marie-Antoinette, frustrated and bored, was no longer

42

able to escape to her Petit Trianon. As for Madame Elizabeth, she must occasionally have received visits from her former companion, for Marie Grosholtz and her uncle were now near neighbours. From this period dates Marie's waxwork group of the King and Queen with their two children, originally exhibited at the Petit Trianon at Versailles, and which can still be seen at the modern Exhibition in London. Disappointing as a work of art, there is, nevertheless, pathos in this stiff, formal group, with its heavy-featured King and plump, petulant Queen. Many generations have gazed at it; the powdered nobility of Versailles with their quizzing-glasses, the Revolutionary crowds in Curtius's Salon, and how many sightseers in how many towns and villages during the thirty years during which Madame Tussaud toured Great Britain with her travelling show! And there they still sit, in London, the amiable, weary King and his capricious Queen, while the plebeian traffic of Marylebone Road roars and rumbles outside.

CHAPTER FOUR

'AUX ARMES, CITOYENS!'

From the autumn of 1789 to the summer of 1791 there was a period of comparative calm. The National Assembly, which had now moved to Paris with the King, passed a series of reforming enactments which the King, with varying degrees of reluctance, accepted. In June, 1790, nobility was abolished. In July came the Church Establishment Bill, which ruled that all bishops and clergy should be appointed by local election, and rearranged the old dioceses and parishes. There was considerable opposition by some of the clergy to Article XXI, which required every beneficed priest to take a solemn oath 'to be loyal to the nation, the law and the King, and to uphold by every means in his power the Constitution decreed by the National Assembly'. Although he sanctioned this decree, Louis disliked it intensely, and his patronage of non-juring priests, i.e. those who refused to take the oath, was one of the many acts which finally turned the people against him.

However, for nearly two years there were no major disturbances, and Marie's account of this period contains little but casual gossip about the distinguished visitors to her uncle's Salon, varied by an occasional reference to such events as the great Fête of Federation of July, 1790, the first anniversary of the fall of the Bastille. An amphitheatre was built in the Champs de Mars surrounding the 'Altar of the Country' and the *Memoirs* state: 'Twelve thousand workmen were at first employed in the requisite preparations: but soon, they not being found sufficient, the Parisians voluntarily lent their aid, and the spectacle became one of the most interesting and extraordinary kind;

ecclesiastics, military, and people of all classes, from the highest to the lowest, wielded the spade and pick-axe, whilst even elegant females lent their aid, and, consistent with the feeling of the period, Madame Tussaud assisted and trundled a barrow in the Champs de Mars.'

On the appointed day an immense procession marched to the amphitheatre. The streets were packed, handkerchiefs fluttered from every window, hundreds of women walked in procession dressed in white and tricolour sashes.

After Talleyrand, the cynical Bishop of Autun, had celebrated Mass, Lafayette, dismounting from his charger, mounted the stage to receive the commands of the King. As thousands of swords glittered in the sunlight the people heard the King solemnly vow: 'I, King of the French, swear to employ the power delegated to me by the constitutional act of the State in maintaining the constitution decreed by the National Assembly and accepted by me.' Marie-Antoinette also made one of her timely appearances on the balcony with the Dauphin in her arms, and was rapturously received.

It must have seemed to Marie Grosholtz that the worst troubles were over. Royal visitors continued to patronize the Salon, and came in for Marie's sly comments. There was, for instance, Marie-Antoinette's brother, Joseph II, Emperor of Germany, whom Dr. Curtius escorted through this Museum. Marie says: 'The Emperor, appearing to be delighted with all he saw, asked Mr. Curtius if he had anything in hand at the time, expressing a wish to visit the studio . . . but as he was conducting Joseph II downstairs his olfactory nerves were greeted by a scent, to a German ever welcome, and he lifted up his hands and threw back his head, exclaiming, "Oh, Mein Gott, there is *Sauerkraut*!" No sooner was the door opened, discovering the family of M. Curtius at dinner over the tempting *Sauerkraut*, than the Emperor exclaimed, "Oh, do let me partake," when, *instanter*, a napkin, plate, etc., were produced, and His Imperial Majesty seated himself at the table . . . consumed his own share of a large dish of *Sauerkraut*, and then said "There! Now I have dined." '

At the suggestion of Brissot, now Mayor of Paris, Louis began to move more freely among the people, visiting factories, exhibitions and hospitals, and seeming to show a genuine interest in the affairs of the nation. But if the King seemed ready to accept the new situation there were strong forces at Court working for a restoration of royal absolutism. The Queen in particular favoured such men as the reactionary Marquis de Bouillé, who wanted the Royal Family to escape to Metz, where, with the backing of an Austrian army, they could, it was hoped, dictate their own terms to the Assembly.

Meanwhile Mirabeau, the adroit politician and popular orator, had been reduced to such straits by luxurious living that he was eager to get royal employment, if only to pay his debts. Eventually he became Court adviser at a salary of £300 a week, his advice being contained in a series of letters urging the King to accept the Constitution, stand by the people and their representatives and by so doing retain his popularity and power. The letters had little effect, and when, in April, 1791, Mirabeau died, worn out both by work and dissipation, his advice, if ever considered, was soon forgotten. Marie says that the funeral of the 'Demosthenes of France', whom she had seen so often drunk at her uncle's table, 'exceeded anything of the kind she had ever witnessed'.

With Mirabeau's death the last temporizing influence upon the Court ceased, and the Queen, ardently supported by her friends, continued to make plans for the Royal Family to escape from Paris to Metz. She was encouraged by the fact that on February 4th the King's pious aunts, Madame Victoria and Madame Adelaide, had succeeded in leaving the country for Rome. The Civil Constitution of the Church had been too much for them. Then in April the King and Queen were prevented by the people from taking their usual summer holiday at St. Cloud. Their coach was stopped by a suspicious crowd. In vain Lafayette arrived and pleaded with them. The people were

46

adamant, and the Royal Family were forced to leave their coach and return to their apartments in the hated Tuileries. Probably it was this final frustration which decided the King to accept the Queen's plan for escape in disguise.

The plot was carefully laid with the help of several close friends, led by the handsome young Swedish nobleman, Count Axel de Fersen, an officer in the Royal-Suedois Regiment. Marie-Antoinette indulged a romantic friendship for the melancholy Count, and it seems certain that he was in love with her. She also kept in touch with her brother, Leopold II of Austria, who promised, in a letter dated ten days before the flight, that if it succeeded and the Royal Family reached safety, money and troops would be at their disposal, if necessary to march on Paris. None the less, the King and Queen had to draw deeply from their own financial resources and those of their friends. Fersen contributed £30,000 from his own fortune, and borrowed £15,000 from Quentin Crauford, a wealthy Scotsman. The King also drew heavily from the Civil List—over £139,000. There were many hitches and last-minute cancellations, but on June 20th Fersen decided that the time had come for the Royal Family to make their bid for freedom.

At a quarter past ten at night Fersen, dressed as coachman, brought the hired carriage round to an unguarded door in the south-east corner of the Palace. One by one, in order not to arouse suspicion, he picked up the Royal fugitives and drove them by a roundabout route to the barrière Saint-Martin, where a large travelling coach was waiting. The Queen passed as the children's governess, 'Madame Rocher'; the King was disguised as a valet, 'Durand'; the little Dauphin was dressed as a girl, Madame Elizabeth as a nursery-maid, while the children's real governess, Madame de Tourzel, became 'the Baronne de Korff'. Three Life Guards, disguised as servants, rode beside the coach or preceded it as couriers. They left the barrier unsuspected, and when Fersen returned to Paris he found that all was calm. The escape was not known to the Municipality until six in the morning. 'Lafayette was one of the first who heard of the King's departure, and ordered his aide-de-camp to start immediately in pursuit of the fugitives. . . . The sensation throughout Paris was indescribable; all the shops were shut, the tocsin was sounded, and the drums beat to arms; a general apprehension seemed to persuade the populace that Louis would soon return with an army, composed of emigrants and foreigners, and wreak a dreadful vengeance upon the people of Paris.'

Meanwhile, the great travelling coach lumbered on towards the frontier. At Châlons Louis incautiously put his head out of the window and was recognized, but the Mayor, who was a Royalist, prevented any measures being taken. The King, now feeling sure he was safe, insisted on stopping for a meal, though the rest of the party were all for continuing non-stop to the frontier. Then, at St. Ménehould a man named Drouet, an ardent revolutionist, recognized the monarch and galloped off to warn the citizens of Varennes, through which the coach would have to pass. The fugitives might still have passed through Varennes in safety but for an unexpected delay. The fresh horses which they had arranged to have meet them near Varennes were not at the appointed place, and half an hour was wasted in looking for them. This gave Drouet time to reach Varennes and warn the authorities. The coach was stopped, passports were demanded and the party, exhausted by their twenty-four-hour journey, forced to alight.

The bid had failed; and yet a hundred yards away were the horses and a company of Hussars who could have carried the fugitives to safety.

So, once again under guard, the Royal Family made their entry into Paris. Marie Grosholtz, in her account of the flight, says little which is not known from other sources, but she adds a typical comment on the Bourbon appetite, which she had had ample opportunities of studying: '. . . It was generally supposed that, had not the King insisted on stopping to dine, he would not have been recognized, and must certainly have escaped; the Queen, and the rest of the party, were for proceeding without delay, but the Bourbons ever had good appetites, and were

LEFT *Portrait of Joseph Tussaud the eldest son of Madame Tussaud*
RIGHT *Portrait of Francis Tussaud, the youngest son of Madame Tussaud and from whom the family descends*
BELOW *Bernard Tussaud and his brother Angelo Tussaud, the great-great-grandsons of Madame Tussaud*

ABOVE   *The French Royal Family. Left to right: Madame Tussaud,
Marie-Antoinette, the Dauphin, Voltaire, the Princess Royale,
Louis XVI, Coquette*
BELOW   *Death masks. Left to right: Fouquier-Tinville, Hebert,
Robespierre, Carrier*

generally disposed to indulge them. . . . Monsieur de Provence [Louis XVIII], though possessing a still higher reputation than any of his family for his gastronomic powers, yet . . . did not retard his journey by stopping to display his prowess . . . [but at Versailles] so ardently did he patronize the larder or pantry that he used frequently to pay it private special visits, and stuff various good things into his pocket to eat whilst out riding . . . [and Marie remembers] to have seen the gravy dropping from his coat-skirts, as, most vexatiously, it oozed through his pockets, owing to the provender not having been wrapped with sufficient caution.'

She goes on to describe the rise of a new republican spirit in Paris after the King's return, and of the formation, at this time, of various political clubs some of which were openly republican in spirit. Among them there was the famous Jacobin Club, which Dr. Curtius joined.

For the next few weeks the capital was full of nervous rumours. The King was believed to be planning another flight. Lafayette was urged to call out the National Guard, but refused. Then there was discontent among unemployed workmen, and some, it was feared, were conspiring with elements within the National Guard. In the middle of this period of anxiety, the second Lord Palmerston, who happened to be in Paris, recorded in his diary a significant ceremony. On July 11th the remains of Voltaire were transferred to the Pantheon to rest beside Mirabeau. His Lordship wrote: 'A figure of Voltaire, very like him, in a gown, was carried first, sitting in an elbow chair, and afterwards came the coffin in a very fine triumphal car drawn by twelve beautiful grey horses four abreast. The coffin was covered, and over it a waxen figure was laid on a bed.'

Although this incident is not mentioned by Marie in her *Memoirs*, it seems likely that these wax figures came from the Salon of Curtius. Solemn crowds followed the cortège of the national hero who had suffered under the aristocracy, been banished by the monarchy, and before his death had returned in triumph to the capital to be honoured by his countrymen.

Six days later blood flowed in the Champs de Mars and the Revolution, which had seemed to hang fire for nearly two years, moved on towards its climax. Two of the most prominent Republican Clubs, the Cordeliers and the Jacobins, published a Petition for signature in the Champs de Mars, condemning the King as a 'perjured traitor and fugitive', demanding his abdication and the convening of 'a new constitutional body which may, in a genuinely national manner, try the criminal; above all to replace him and to organize a new executive power'. At the Altar of the Country on the Champs de Mars 6,000 people signed the Petition—men and women, old and young, from the educated middle class to illiterate workmen who could only make a cross on the paper.

But the National Assembly were not prepared to go so far. The Petition alarmed them. They wanted a compromise; still to retain the King, but to limit his power. The Assembly had lost the faith of the people, and, realizing this, acted as frightened men often do in such circumstances—by appealing to force. Martial law was declared, the red flag—a symbol then of authority, not of revolt—flew from the Town Hall. In the evening Lafayette's troops marched into the Champs de Mars with cavalry, infantry and guns. The angry crowd roared, 'Down with the Red Flag!' Brickbats flew, and the soldiers fired, first over the heads of the crowd, then into it. Twelve citizens were killed and over thirty wounded.

The Deputies, far from deprecating this slaughter of defenceless people, triumphed in it. Citizens who dared to criticize the Assembly, Lafayette or the National Guard were arrested, among them Marat. Robespierre and his fellow Jacobins were under suspicion; and some went into hiding. But no tyrannical decrees could damp the determination of the citizens, or efface the memory of the Massacre of the Champs de Mars. The dethronement of the King, though it might be delayed, could not now be averted.

The first task of the Assembly after the Massacre was to draw up a Constitution which would be acceptable to Louis and the foreign powers which might threaten France. In September it was drawn up and formally accepted by the King, although most of the Assembly realized that its reforms fell far short of popular demand. The Great Powers received it with cold suspicion. Gustavus of Sweden stated bluntly that he did not consider Louis was a free agent. Katherine of Russia reserved judgement. The Elector of Treves and Metz, to whom many of the noble *émigrés* had fled, returned evasive answers. The conviction grew in France that sooner or later foreign armies, led by Leopold of Austria, the Queen's brother, would invade the country with the object of restoring the former power of the discredited monarchy. The Comte de Narbonne, Minister for War, with General Dumouriez, prepared to arm the nation; an army of 100,000 men was to be assembled on the Rhine. People talked openly of the coming war.

The King was now a bitterly despondent man, forced to make concessions which limited his powers, and enduring repeated humiliations at the hand of such men as Chabot (who entered the royal presence wearing his hat), yet realizing that the people could never trust him again. There is a pathetic passage in Marie's *Memoirs* in which the King confides in General Dumouriez: 'Yesterday evening I went to the window towards the court, just to take a little air, and a gunner of the guard addressed me, "How I should like to see your head stuck on the point of my bayonet!" In that horrid garden you see, on one side, a man mounted on a chair, reading aloud the most infamous calumnies against us; on the other, an abbé, or a military man, dragged through one of the basins, overwhelmed with abuse, and beaten, while others are quietly playing at ball, or walking to and fro. What an abode! And what a people!'

Meanwhile, the Salon of Curtius continued to be one of the most popular entertainments of Paris, though the wax figures of the revolutionary leaders, orators and statesmen had begun to replace the aristocrats and court ladies whom the public once paid to see. For Curtius, now a prominent though not ardent member of the Jacobin Club, was cultivating the people's favourites. Marie saw them all, and as they pass in procession through the pages of her book, we see them too, through those observant eyes and keen brain which retained every physical detail. Here is the giant figure of Danton: '. . . His exterior was almost enough to scare a child; his features were large and harsh . . . his head immense . . . his voice was such as might be expected to proceed from so tremendous a frame.'

And yet, Marie tells us, 'notwithstanding his formidable appearance and the thunder of his tones when speaking, he could be very mild and pleasing in his manners.'

He would often talk to Marie and 'was very pressing that she should attend all the Revolutionary fêtes'. And here is Marat, Curtius's countryman, the brilliant Swiss physician, revolutionary journalist, fierce orator and uncompromising enemy of aristocracy: 'He was very short—with very small arms, one of which was feeble from some natural defect, and appeared lame; his complexion was sallow, of a greenish hue; his eyes dark and piercing; his hair was wild, and raven black; his countenance had a fierce aspect; he was slovenly in his dress, and even dirty in his person. . . . His command of words appeared unlimited; they flowed from his lips as if they came by inspiration, and from his small person thundered forth a voice which would have befitted a stronger man. Whilst he was displaying his powers of oratory his eyes glared as if they would start from their sockets, and his gesticulations, which were quite theatrical, resembled those of one who was under the influence of some demonical possession.'

It was men such as these who forged the weapons of Revolution. It was Danton's oratory, Marat's inflammatory journalism, which fanned the public's anger with their Deputies as the National Assembly stumbled into an ill-prepared war against Austria, thence to disaster and defeat. War had been declared on March 20th and Dumouriez had begun by sending two columns into Belgium in the hope of starting an anti-Austrian revolt. But at this stage the French troops were ill-disciplined, inexperienced, and badly led, and both columns were put to flight. In the rout, Dillon, one of the generals in command, was murdered by his own men. Paris received the news with dismay and anger. Treachery was suspected and again the people turned against the King and his Ministers.

Dumouriez, whose unpopularity was increased by his having supported the King, belonged to a party called the Gironde, from the Department of France from which most of its members came. It represented the most influential body of Deputies within the National Assembly and was led by a Monsieur Roland, little-known husband of a much more famous wife, Madame Roland. Roland remonstrated with Dumouriez for having spent 100,000 francs on his private pleasures, whereupon Dumouriez broke with the Girondists, who were supported by the Jacobin Club and many of the newspapers. Dumouriez responded by taking action against the journalists, one of whom was Marat. Already a decree had been issued against him for inciting the people against the King and Royal Family in his *l'Ami du Peuple* and it was probably at this time that Marie Grosholtz and her uncle received an unexpected visit from the demagogue—with his carpet bag. The *Memoirs* state: '. . . He came on a Saturday night, and requested an asylum, having in his hand his carpet bag, containing what few clothes and linen he required. He was received, and remained until the following Saturday. . . . He used to write almost the whole day, in a corner, with a little lamp, and on one occasion he came up to Madame Tussaud and gave her a tap on the shoulder, with such roughness as caused her to shudder, saying, "There, Mademoiselle, it is not for ourselves that I and my fellow labourers are working, but it is for you, and your children and your children's children. As to ourselves, we shall in all probability not live to see the fruits of our exertions," adding that "all the aristocrats must be killed." . . .'

And Marie adds the surprising statement: 'He made a

calculation of how many people could be killed in one day, and decided that the number might amount to 26,000.'

More congenial is a mildly lunatic figure with the extraordinary name of Anarchasis Kloots (Marie spells it Cloots). Even to revolutionary France, which threw up many eccentrics, he was a bit too much. On June 19th this French-speaking Dutch Baron from Cleves walked into the House of National Assembly accompanied by thirty-six so-called 'foreigners' dressed in various national costumes borrowed from the Opera House. In a gloriously wild harangue, accompanied by frantic gestures, he spoke as 'the orator of the human race to the Legislature of the human race. My heart is France and my soul *san-sculotte*.' He also called himself 'the member for the Universe' and talked of France as the 'new Mother of the Peoples'.

Curtius, from whom Kloots borrowed money, knew the Baron well. So did Marie, who describes him as 'tall, thin, and pale. . . . Cloots was always melancholy, on account of the loss of his wife, which induced him to travel'. But such romantic diversions were becoming rare. The Assembly had to concern itself with the hard realities of war abroad and civil strife at home. In June a crisis arose over the proposal to dismiss 1,200 of the National Guardsmen whom the King was allowed to keep in Paris on his establishment; they were suspected of being too royalist in sympathy. At the same time it was proposed that National Guardsmen from the provinces, who were generally anti-royalist, should be allowed to train at a special camp near Paris before leaving for the front. The Assembly liked the idea, as it augmented their power. The republicans liked it because it diminished the power of the King. But influential sections of the Paris municipalities were against the decree, believing it would mean the virtual disarming of Paris and the loss of control over their own destinies. Encouraged by this opposition, the King intervened with the Royal veto—another cause of popular discontent. A succession of dismissals, resignations and fresh ministerial appointments followed, until by the end of the month the Government was in the hands of political nonentities—mere Court nominees without public confidence.

By instinct, the people's resentment was focused on the stronghold of the hated Austrian interest—the Tuileries. On June 20th a large armed crowd gathered and marched on the Palace. They invaded the Parliament House and made threatening speeches against the King, inveighed against the dismissal of the 'patriot ministers' and paraded through the Hall of Assembly crying, 'Down with the Veto!' Then they broke into the Tuileries Gardens and found their way into the Palace. Shouting, smashing their way in with hatchets, the mob surged into the Royal apartments, and this time there was no protection for the Royal Family. Louis was forced into a window embrasure with a few friends and officers of the Royal household.

'No veto,' roared the crowd. 'No priests! No aristocrats!'

Legendre, one of the leaders of the mob, stepped forward and demanded the confirmation of the vetoed decree. Louis replied with dignity and courage that that was for his Ministers to decide, and the crowd responded with cries of 'Long live the Nation!'

'I am its best friend,' said Louis.

'Then prove it!' demanded one of the mob, holding towards the King a red cap on the end of a pike. The red cap, the famous *bonnet rouge*, had become the symbol of liberty. Louis reached forward, took the cap and set it on his head. The crowd cheered, and after a time were induced to leave.

Still the people were not satisfied. They distrusted the King, for had he not already tried to escape from Paris and induce foreign armies to invade France? They distrusted the National Assembly, for was it not still temporizing with the monarchy? One last resort remained—make an armed attack on the Tuileries, destroy the Court faction, arrest and depose the King, and force the people's representatives to set up a true republic. The people of Paris began to arm and prepare. From

55

the country districts towards the capital marched the Fédérés, the provincial companies of the National Guard who were coming to the camp near Paris to train before leaving for the front. These young soldiers made valuable allies for the Parisian citizens.

Meanwhile, Danton thundered out his splendid oratory and Marat and the other Jacobin leaders talked, warned, and harangued the people. On August 3rd, forty-seven out of the forty-eight Paris *Sections* sent a Petition to the House demanding that Louis give up the throne, and the summoning of a National Convention. The petition was referred to committee and shelved. The revolutionaries tried again on August 8th, calling for the impeachment of Lafayette, who was no longer the popular hero of 1789, but was too closely associated with the King. Again the motion was defeated. The Commune, i.e. the organized *Sections*, or districts, of the Paris Municipality, decided that only force could now liberate them from a treacherous King and complete the revolution which had begun three years earlier.

Their determination was increased when they read the arrogant Manifesto published by the Duke of Brunswick at Metz, but undoubtedly drafted at the Tuileries. The Prussian Duke declared that he intended to march on Paris, 'to put an end to anarchy, to stop the attacks on the throne and altar, and restore to the King the safety and liberty of which he had been deprived.' Any civilian opposing the invading armies was to be executed and his home burned. Vengeance would be meted out to anyone offering violence to the King and Queen. Any National Guardsman found in arms would be treated as a traitor. Paris or any other city offering resistance would be blasted by cannon shot.

To this characteristically Prussian document the Parisians' answer was to arm and prepare. From the provinces contingents of the National Guard, the citizen army which had been formed in 1789, marched towards the capital. Among them were 615 young National Guardsmen from Marseilles, carefully

56

picked for their fitness and high morale. They were called 'Les Marseillois', and as they marched into the capital on July 30th they sang a new marching-song composed by Roget de Lisle. Now Paris heard it for the first time. It caught at the hearts of the anxious crowds, its lilt gave them courage, its words were a challenge:

> *Allons, enfants de la Patrie!*
> *Le jour de gloire est arrivé. . . .*

Quickly the words were taken up and the thrilling chorus was roared out to the tramp of marching feet:

> *Aux armes, citoyens!*
> *Formez vos battaillons!*
> *Marchons! Marchons! . . .*

Marie heard it on that fateful night of August 9th, when the insurrectional Commune sat in consultation in the Hotel de Ville, and the Tuileries prepared to resist the coming attack. That night, she says in her *Memoirs*, 'the tocsin sounded, the *generale* was beaten; the shoutings of the populace, and all the bells at once clanging, formed a horrible discord, and the terror inspired by that awful night . . . was beyond all description.'

Marie had cause for anxiety, for among the Swiss guard who defended the Tuileries were five of her kinsmen, two uncles and three brothers.

The Tuileries was garrisoned by 3,000 men, including 900 veteran Swiss soldiers, 900 gendarmes, 2,000 National Guards (though their loyalty was doubtful) and several hundred royalist volunteers. Against them the revolutionary leaders were preparing to throw an undisciplined mob of civilians stiffened by half-trained volunteers. The attack might possibly have failed but for the weakness and treachery of those responsible for the King's safety. Mandat, responsible for the defence of the Palace, was lured to the Hotel de Ville, arrested, and murdered. Roederer, *Procureur* of the Paris Department, told the King that there would be no attack, then persuaded the Royal Family to place themselves under the protection of the Assembly. But Louis did not cancel the order to defend the Palace, and when the mob surged forward across the *carousel* and the Swiss opened fire, most of the defenders did not know that their King had deserted the garrison. The National Guard within the Palace went over to the people as was expected, but the veteran Swiss Guardsmen, including Marie's kinsmen, fought on. At a crisis in the struggle, Louis, who hated violence, ordered that the Swiss should lay down their arms and retire to their barracks. At such a moment the command was fatal. Thrown into confusion, their cohesion broken, the Guard were split into isolated groups. Still they fought until most of them were cut to pieces. Some escaped. Some climbed on to the ornamental statuary in the garden, but were prodded with bayonets until they came down and were then slaughtered. By morning only 300 out of the original 600 were still alive.

The *Memoirs* describe how Marie Grosholtz, unable to go out on the streets, was compelled to wait at home in terrible suspense while '. . . every hour, the reports which kept arriving told a tale of murder and horrors. . . . The night was comparatively still, but ever and anon, a shot was heard and the huzzas of the rioters still insulted the ears of the peaceable'.

Next morning Marie still had no news of the fate of her relatives. Accompanied by a woman friend, she made her way to the Tuileries by a circuitous route, avoiding the main streets, where rioting and looting still went on. At last the two ladies arrived at the Tuileries Gardens 'which had so often been the scene of innocent joy and revelry . . . but now, alas! how bitter was the contrast! Wherever the eye turned it fell upon many a corpse . . . the beautiful gravel walks were stained with blood . . .'

Marie wandered through the trampled gardens and silent courts, past the burned-out barracks, going from body to body, fearful of what she might find. Yet when, at the end of her quest, she had still failed to recognize the faces of any of her relatives she began to have a little hope. Some of the Swiss had escaped. Perhaps her uncles and brothers were among them? But when she reached her uncle's house again the blow fell— positive news that all the kinsmen for whom she sought had died defending the Tuileries.

CHAPTER FIVE

THE TERROR

After forty-eight hours, the Royal Family was taken from the House of Assembly to the Temple. The Commune insisted on this. The Assembly, dominated by the moderate Girondists, wanted to instal them in the Luxembourg Palace; they were still sympathetic to Louis and were not, at this stage, willing to punish him. But the Commune, representing the citizens of Paris, had shown that they were not to be trifled with. To them the King was a perjured traitor, worthy only to be treated as a prisoner, so it was to the grim baronial tower of the Temple with its narrow windows and deep ditch that the King and Queen were finally committed; they never left it except to go to their trial and execution.

There was, says Marie Grosholtz, such intense interest in the prisoners, that owners of houses overlooking the gardens were able to let their lodgings at a high rate, 'numbers of people paying for admission to those rooms from the windows of which they could obtain a view of the King and his family walking in the Temple Garden'. She admits she went herself, 'but felt so hurt at seeing them in such a situation' that she never again desired to witness their misfortunes. Marie herself was imprisoned, with her mother and aunt, on suspicion of being royalists. They were denounced, she says, 'by a man who used to play the part of a *grimacier* and was a dancer, in a little theatre near the house of Dr Curtius'. No doubt if the Doctor had been in Paris at the time he could have prevented this with a well-placed bribe, or a discreet word in the right quarters; but, unfortunately for his sisters and niece, he was 'with the Army on the Rhine' on some mysterious business which Marie does not clearly specify.

So at midnight gendarmes arrived at the Salon and the frightened women were bundled into a *fiacre* and carried off to the prison of La Force. They were confined in a small room with twenty other women. One of them attracted Marie's interest because of her spirit and gaiety, an attractive, vigorous woman with a little girl; a woman who 'never gave way to despondency. . . . She did all in her power to infuse life and spirit into her suffering companions, exhorting them to patience, and endeavouring to cheer them. When the great bolts were undrawn, a general shuddering was excited among the prisoners [but this woman] would rally them by bidding them have courage; and it often happened that the alarm was merely caused by the doors being opened for persons to bring in food for the prisoners.'

The woman was Josephine de Beauharnais, later to become the wife of Napoleon.

Every week the women were compelled to have their hair closely cut, so that their heads might be in fit trim for the guillotine, for which they were told to prepare themselves. The food was abominable, and as no bedding was available, the prisoners slept upon straw. 'Several ladies sent their ear-rings and other jewels to be sold, so that with the proceeds they might procure more nourishment than the gaol allowance afforded.'

But Josephine, with her little girl, always lived upon the prison fare. Eventually, through the influence of General Kleber, in whose army Curtius was serving, Marie and her family were set free, but Madame de Beauharnais was not released until many months later.

Marie was lucky to escape, for the attitude of the Parisian mob towards suspected royalists was one of hysterical anger. There had been mass arrests, and the people feared that, with so many men away at the front, the capital would be at the mercy of the prisoners if they managed to break out of the ill-guarded, overcrowded prisons. The leaders of the Commune, particularly Marat and Danton, did nothing to allay this fear, and when, in September, mobs entered the jails and massacred the prisoners, the authorities did not intervene. Some openly expressed their approval of these 'acts of revolutionary justice'.

There is an atmosphere of sickening horror about the September Massacres. Perhaps it is because they were carried out, not by professional killers, cut-throats and ruffians, but by ordinary citizens. They were the men who dragged twenty priests from the carriages which were taking them to the prison at the Abbaye of Saint-Germain-des-Pres, and murdered them. At the Châtelet they killed 215 thieves and debtors; in another prison 170 boys and girls; at Salpétrière, thirty-five women. About 1,300 people were slaughtered, most of them non-political prisoners. Drink was provided by the *Sections* for the killers, and a fee of 24*s*. per man.

In some prisons the victims were given a rough-and-ready trial. After a few questions and answers, sentence was pronounced. If the prisoner was judged to be innocent, a rare occurrence, he or she was given liberty. If guilty, they were handed over to the mob waiting outside with bloody pikes to stab and hack them to death. One of the prisoners, the aged Sombreuil, ex-Governor of the Invalides, was saved by the intervention of his lovely daughter who 'rushed from the prison, amidst the weapons of destruction, and, in an agony of grief . . . pleaded with such piteous eloquence . . . that the assassins halted awhile, and, handing to her a pot filled with gore, they cried "Drink, then, the blood of aristocrats." The heroic girl did as was required and saved her father.'

So writes Marie in her *Memoirs* and then goes on to describe one of the most harrowing of her own experiences, though only the first of many. One of the close friends of Madame Elizabeth, whom Marie had often met at Versailles, was the beautiful Princess de Lamballe, only twenty-four years of age. The Princess was a captive in one of the prisons attacked by the mob during the September Massacres. After a rough-and-ready 'trial', the verdict of 'Guilty' was pronounced, and the dreadful order came: 'Let Madame be set at liberty!' Immediately she was thrust into the crowd and hewn to pieces, her body mutilated, and her head first taken to the Temple and shown to the King and Queen, then carried to Marie Grosholtz, where, in the words of the *Memoirs*, '... the savage murderers stood over her, whilst she, shrinking with horror, was compelled to take a cast from the features of the unfortunate princess.'

Typical of this period is a horrible story told by Audot, who, when an old man of eighty, remembered, as a child, seeing two piles of dead, priests on one side, laymen on the other. As the blood was being washed from the pavement, the onlookers stood back, leaving a gap, and said, 'Let the child have a look.'

Yet most of the perpetrators of these crimes were not hardened criminals, but middle-aged tradesmen—hat-makers, jewellers, cobblers and cabinet-makers—urged on by fear and hate.

This cruelty was inspired, as it usually is, by fear; fear of treachery, and fear of the victorious Allied armies under the Duke of Brunswick which had taken Longwy and Verdun and were now within 140 miles of Paris. A circular directed at this time to all town halls from the *Salut Public* contains this statement: 'A part of the ferocious conspirators detained in the prisons have been put to death by the people; and we cannot doubt the whole nation, driven to the edge of ruin by such endless series of treasons, will make haste to adopt this means of public salvation; and all Frenchmen will cry as the men of Paris: We go to fight the enemy: but we will not leave robbers behind us, to butcher our wives and children.' Among the signatures to this terrible document is that of Marat—'Friend of the People.'

Such outrages can only be understood in the broader perspective of national danger. The red flag flew from the Hôtel de Ville. Montmartre was being fortified. Every day thousands of volunteers marched northward to join the ill-organized, ill-armed forces which were all that stood between Paris and the enemy.

Meanwhile Lafayette had fled to Austria, and General Dumouriez had been appointed to the chief command of the armed forces.

Yet, even while the Prussians were advancing on Paris and the rioters were attacking the prisons, France was electing a new National Convention, which met for the first time on September 20th. Among the new representatives were several Englishmen who had been invited to become honorary citizens of France because their writings had 'prepared the road for liberty'. They were Joseph Priestley, James Macintosh, David Williams, Thomas Clarkson, Thomas Paine and William Wilberforce. However, only Tom Paine, who had just published the second part of his *Rights of Man*, took his seat in the new Assembly. The others, while accepting the honour, preferred to remain at home.

On the very same day the troops under Dumouriez were winning the vital battle of Valmy, which has been described as the Thermopylæ of France. Dumouriez had succeeded in blocking the passes through the Argonne, so that for weary days Brunswick's Prussians, with their *émigré* allies, had stumbled and floundered through the rain-drenched forests, unable to force a passage.

Wearied by forced marches, weakened by malaria, Brunswick's troops were compelled to fight Dumouriez on ground of his own choosing, and a few miles west of Sainte-Ménehould the Republican armies triumphantly beat back the Prussian assault with cries of '*Vive la France!*' and '*Vive la Nation!*' The bells of Paris pealed and clashed and the citizens cheered with joy and relief at the amazing, almost incredible news—that the enemy was retreating to the frontier. The Republic had been saved.

Dumouriez, his earlier indiscretions forgotten, became hero of the hour. He returned to Paris to be fêted and acclaimed, while Collot d'Herbois, one of the leading Jacobins, addressed him in a style of lofty panegyric. Marie, who had met both of them at her uncle's house, describes the general as 'a short man, but

very stoutly made, energetic in his manner, and full of animation. He is supposed to have offered his services to almost every
power in Europe; but such was his varying character that no one
liked to trust him. . . . He was fifty years of age when the
Revolution occurred, but had not lost any of the ardour and
activity of youth. . . . He died in London in the year 1823.'

But her most penetrating comments are on Collot d'Herbois,
to whom both she and her uncle were indebted for his having
persuaded them 'to style themselves in their passports as
Alsatians, and not Swiss, and even procuring them a false
register to that effect'. The Swiss were not popular in France
at this time. Collot d'Herbois, says Marie, had been an actor
'and had played at several places; amongst the rest, Lyons,
where, having been hissed, he imbibed the deepest hatred for
the inhabitants, and vowed that he would one day be revenged
upon them; and fully he kept his promise. He was sent there to
purify the people, to make them feel the effects of the Revolution, and to purge that city of aristocrats. The guillotine was not
deemed rapid enough to satisfy his thirst for blood, and he had
recourse to artillery, and poured grape-shot into the masses of
his victims which he had selected for destruction'. And she
finishes her thumbnail sketch of this monster with the words:
'banished to Cayenne . . . and the climate not agreeing with him,
he caught a violent fever, which he aggravated by drinking a
quart of brandy at once, and died in the greatest agonies.'

Now that the danger of foreign intervention had passed, the
Convention decided early in 1793, to try the King. After Louis
had appeared before the Bar of the House and made his defence,
the Deputies were divided. Many, including most of the Girondins, were for caution; Louis must be punished, but not executed. The other party, led by the Jacobins, wanted the extreme
penalty. From eight o'clock on the evening of January 16th
until the same time on the following day the Deputies voted,
some accompanying their vote with speeches. It was a fantastic
scene, with one end of the great Hall of Assembly fitted up as a
lounge buffet, where ladies in attractive negligées sat at tables

talking and drinking with their friends, while below them each of the Deputies mounted the rostrum in turn to register his vote. There was heavy betting on the outcome. Here and there Deputies fell asleep in their chairs, while some of the scrutineers, sympathetic towards the King, surreptitiously destroyed voting-papers. But all such attempts were in vain. When the result was announced there was a majority of seventy votes in favour of the King's death.

The day of the execution, Marie tells us, was one of the most melancholy and imposing she ever remembered to have seen: 'Every shop, and even every window, was closed, and people mostly retired to the backs of the houses, along the line by which the dreadful cavalcade had to pass . . . a solemn silence reigned, as the carriage, containing the royal victim, passed between the lines of troops, which were under arms; cannon was also planted so as to be in readiness, in case any attempt at rescue should occur.'

The Bourbons never lacked personal courage and, like Charles I, Louis XVI met his death with heroic dignity. He addressed the people from the scaffold, swearing that he was innocent of the charges laid against him, and forgiving those responsible for his death. Then the drums were ordered to beat, drowning the monarch's voice, and Louis laid his head in the lunette. As the great knife fell, the Abbé Edgeworth, who accompanied the King to the scaffold, cried out, 'Son of St. Louis, ascend to Heaven!' The executioner showed the bleeding head to the crowd, which roared, 'Vive la Nation!' and dipped their hand-kerchiefs in the royal blood. Later the leonine Danton, in a defiant speech, shouted: 'The coalized kings threaten us; we hurl at their feet, as gage of battle, the head of a King!'

He had good reason to be jubilant. Following up his victory at Valmy, Dumouriez had invaded the Netherlands. Jemappes (November 6th) and Namur (December 2nd) had added further laurels to his crown, and farther south the forces under Monte-squieu and Anselme had occupied Chambery and Nice. Every-where the armies of the Republic were triumphant, and what had started as an internal revolt became a revolutionary crusade. The Girondin leaders, intoxicated with success, now openly proclaimed that Europe must be set ablaze. 'We must take the offensive,' wrote one of them, Brissot. 'We must electrify every mind, either to make revolution or accept it.'

This is not a history of the Revolution, but the story of one individual who was caught up in it. It is not proposed to follow closely every twist and turn of policy, every rise and fall of parties to and from power, during the turbulent years which passed before Marie Grosholtz left France for England. Instead, our story will describe only events in which she was personally involved, and individuals whose life-strands crossed or were entwined with her own.

Following the declaration of war against England and Holland on February 1st, economic troubles again beset France. The declining value of the *assignats*, the paper currency which had been established, produced a situation in which a pair of shoes worth 5 francs in cash required 700 in *assignats*. Marie declares that she had a room papered with them. Then came fresh military disasters, and the news that 260,000 well-equipped troops were advancing towards France. Dumouriez's stock fell when he lost the Battle of Neerwinden, which he attributed to mismanagement by the Government. Alarmed by rumours that he was negotiating with the Austrians, the Convention sent four commissioners to Dumouriez with instructions to bring him back to Paris, but the general merely checkmated this move by placing the commissioners under arrest.

At about the same time a new party, known as the *Montagne* —an offshoot of the Jacobins—was rapidly gaining popularity, and the Girondins began to lose favour. To make matters worse, some of the provinces came out in open revolt against the Convention, the first being the people of La Vendée, the coastal department lying between La Rochelle and the mouth of the Loire. It is a country of steep hills and narrow valleys, ideal for guerrilla warfare. During the spring of 1793 the revolt spread. From the west the trouble spread to the north, and

soon Limoges, Toulouse and Bordeaux were in arms against the
Government. Marseilles, Nîmes, Toulon, Grenoble and Lyon
followed suit. Much of this resistance was due to the attempts
to raise Republican soldiers for the front; added to this was
religious resentment against the Civil Constitution of the
Church, backed by many of the country gentlemen, who longed
to avenge the death of the King.

Under the stress of these events, the extreme Jacobin party,
the *Montagne*, gained more and more support against the
Girondins, whom they blamed for the perilous state of the
nation. But the blow which did most to unseat their rivals and
place them in power was struck by a young girl, Charlotte Corday, who murdered one of the most popular of the Jacobin
leaders, Jean-Paul Marat. This was an event which Marie had
every reason to remember.

On July 13th gendarmes called at the house of Dr. Curtius
and roughly commanded Marie to accompany them. They drove
to the house of Marat, an old house in the Rue de l'École de
Medecine. Pressing through the great crowd outside, she
entered the house and was led, trembling, into Marat's room. A
group of people were gathered round an object on the floor.
They parted, and Marie saw, lying in a hip-bath, the naked
corpse of the People's Friend, his head thrust back in the agony
of death, a knife wound in his heart.

Charlotte Corday, whom Marie afterwards met in prison, had
travelled from Normandy to Paris with the intention of killing
either Robespierre or Marat. Earlier that day she had bought
a butcher's knife at a shop in the Palais and had then driven to
Marat's lodging and demanded to see him, saying that she had
news from Caen. Marat suffered from a skin disease, contracted, some said, while hiding in the Paris sewers, and could
only obtain relief by lying in a medicated bath. He was doing
so when Charlotte was shown in to him. 'At first [says Marie]
she amused him with an account of the deputies at Caen, when
he said, "They shall go to the guillotine." "To the guillotine,"
she said, and, as he caught up a pencil to write the names of the

offenders, plunged the knife into his heart. "Help, my dear!"
he cried and his housekeeper obeyed the call, and a man who
was near rushed in and knocked down the avenger of her country
with a chair, while the female trampled upon her.'

It was David, the artist, who had given orders for Marie to be
brought to Marat's house. There and then she was commanded
to make a cast of the dead man's features from which he later
painted his famous picture, on which he wrote 'David à Marat',
in recognition of their long-standing friendship. Marie knew
him well. Like most of his fellow revolutionaries, David appears
to have liked Curtius's niece, though his attitude to most of his
fellow artists is summed up in his words: 'If the artists were
fired at with grapeshot there would be no danger of killing a
patriot.' Soon after she had modelled the dead face of Marat,
Marie was called on to perform the same task on the severed
head of Charlotte Corday, who was guillotined shortly after the
murder.

Marie's model of the murdered demagogue was put on exhibition at the Salon of Curtius, where crowds flocked to see it,
among them Robespierre. She says: 'As he quitted the room,
while standing on the steps of the door, he profited by so fine
an opportunity of haranguing the passers by, and soon drew a
crowd around him. "Citizens!" said he, "follow my example;
enter, and see the image of our departed friend, snatched from
us by an assassin's hand, guided by the demon of aristocracy;
but, although the form of Marat is torn from our embrace, long
may his spirit dwell in our minds, and influence our actions!" '

Isidore Maximilien Robespierre, foremost leader of the
Montagne party, could well feel exultant, for he was now rising
to the pinnacle of power, and power to him was life. A patient
schemer, a cold manipulator of men, he could even outwit the
giant Danton, who, for all his ruthless brilliance as an orator and
politician, had roots which went deep down into the coarse clay
of humanity. He had the common weaknesses of the flesh, which
Robespierre never showed openly. Danton could be careless,
impulsive, which Robespierre never was. Danton, in spite of

his crimes, liked his fellow men. Robespierre merely used them.

But for the time being the two worked in comparative harmony.

In early June their rivals, the Girondin Deputies, had been expelled from the Convention. In October twenty-one of them were impeached and brought to trial, on a vague charge of 'belonging to an association for the ruin of the Republic'. After five days, in which little progress had been made, Fouquier-Tinville, the Public Prosecutor, grew impatient and asked why there should be any witnesses, when everyone, including the prisoners themselves, knew the accused to be guilty? Like most political trials, it was a travesty of justice, and when, on the sixth day of the trial a verdict of 'Guilty' was brought in, the prisoners made a demonstration in the court. One stabbed himself in the dock; some fiercely denounced the judges. Others cried 'Vive la République!' The following day they went to the guillotine.

Now the Jacobins were firmly in power, and the Reign of Terror began. On October 16th, a fortnight before the execution of the Girondins, the Queen followed her husband to the scaffold. Marie Grosholtz watched the procession. In the words of the *Memoirs*, 'having heard that the queen's hair had turned grey, and that she was so emaciated and altered as scarcely to be recognizable [Marie] . . . was impelled, by an anxiety once more to see her, as also a curiosity to know if it could be true that so great a change could have taken place in so short a period, and went to a friend's house for the purpose of seeing the unfortunate princess pass on her way to the fatal spot'. As soon, however, as the cavalcade came in sight, Marie Grosholtz fainted. The *Memoirs* continue: 'When the Queen arrived at the place of execution, she cast one sad look towards the Tuileries, and displayed some emotion; but in an instant rallied, and met her fate with unflinching courage.'

Marie-Antoinette was thirty-eight when she died. On the same day Marie Grosholtz was brought to the Madeleine Prison, to which the body had been carried in a handcart, and there forced to make a death-mask of the features she had known so well. That mask can still be seen in the Exhibition in London.

From this point onwards the *Memoirs* become a catalogue of almost unrelieved horror. The Jacobins, determined to put down the revolt of the provinces, which had started in the Vendée Department, took the most extreme measures. We have met Collot d'Herbois, the disappointed actor who revenged himself upon the Lyonnais. Now read Marie's description of Couthon, a friend of Robespierre, who was also sent to punish the people of Lyons for their rebellion: 'He had rather a placid expression, which might have deceived many. He had always a very little pet dog, which he carried with him everywhere, and used to put it in his bosom, urging that his disposition was naturally so social and disposed towards affection, that he found it necessary always to have some object to cherish and caress. He was totally decrepit, and . . . was always obliged to have a servant to carry him, and even place him in his chair. When at Lyons he had himself stationed on an eminence, that he might have a good view of the persons who were put to death, to the number of fifty or sixty a day; besides which he had many of the handsomest houses demolished, and was borne about the city, while with a little silver hammer, which he carried, he gave a knock at the door of the dwelling to be condemned. . . .'

Fouquier-Tinville, Public Prosecutor at the trial of the Girondins, provides another interesting study: 'He was rather tall, his complexion sallow; he was pitted with small pox, had dark hair and a narrow forehead; like most of the functionaries, he dressed in black . . . for Fouquier, pleasure had no attractions; he was generally very abstemious in his diet; his application was intense; and his business consisted in accusing and condemning. The only relaxation which he ever sought was to see his victims suffer whom he had sent to the scaffold; and then his iron features would melt for a moment, and even to soften into a smile, expressive of the delight he experienced in witnessing such spectacles. . . . As he coveted neither comforts nor luxuries, money had no charms for him, therefore he was inaccessible to bribes; as his only enjoyment was that of causing persons to be put to death, and then seeing them die, he knew that wealth would not obtain him that gratification. . . .' Eventually he too was sent to the guillotine, and his death-mask, taken, as usual, by Marie, is now appropriately placed in the Chamber of Horrors.

And there was Carrier, who anticipated the Nazi method of imprisoning their victims in ships, which were then scuttled: '. . . A good-looking man, tall, rather a fine figure, very gentlemanly in his appearance and manners, always dressed extremely well, and was agreeable in conversation. . . . He had other stratagems for the wholesale destruction of his fellow creatures, and had hundreds at a time conducted on board vessels, which were scuttled and by that means sunk . . . at last he has as many as between four and five thousand put to death by various means, consisting of men, women and children; of the latter five hundred at a time were brought out to be shot, the eldest of whom was not fourteen years of age. . . .'

Between July, 1793, and July, 1794, the Jacobins rode in a tide of blood. Paris became sickened by the endless executions; aristocrats went to the guillotine by thousands; politicians rose to power, enjoyed a brief reign in which to accuse, condemn and kill, then were betrayed by their rivals or associates and were slaughtered in their turn. Madame Elizabeth, sister of the late King, the pious Princess whose companion Marie Grosholtz had been in those far-off days before 1789, was a victim. Madame du Barry, unwise enough to return to France from England, was arrested and forced, screaming and struggling, under the fatal knife. Even poor Anarchasis Kloots, 'the orator of the human race', fell a victim, though even on the scaffold 'he quarrelled with a fellow sufferer, and got quite in a passion with him, because he would not be converted to Kloot's way of thinking'.

In March, 1794, it was the turn of Danton and his party, outwitted by Robespierre, who continued implacably to ride the storm. The Revolutionary armies again flung back the invaders. The revolts were quelled. The Convention formally abolished religion, instituted a new Revolutionary Calendar and inaugurated the Age of Reason. But the slaughter of aristocrats did not abate. So incessant were the executions at this period, says Marie, that 'in the Faubourg St. Antoine a channel had been cut from where the guillotine stood, to convey the streams of human gore to the common drain. . . .'

For more than a year these violent and bloody deeds racked the body of France, like a man shaken by fever, with Robespierre, St. Just, Henriot and the other Jacobins as the malignant germs in the national bloodstream. But then the paroxysms slackened and the patient grew quieter; the nation was satiated with bloodshed, and a reaction set in against the Jacobins. Powerful enemies began to speak against Robespierre and his friends, notably Tallien, whose lead was followed by other Deputies. Couthon, in a desperate harangue, did his best to turn public opinion in favour of his friend, but in vain. Robespierre was accused, and ordered to the bar, with his younger brother, Lébas, St. Just and Couthon.

An attempt was made to start an insurrection and rescue the Jacobin leaders. Henriot surrounded the Convention with troops and guns, but the soldiers refused to fire on the Deputies. But the situation was still critical, and Barras, one of the Deputies, collected a number of the National Guard and marched to the Hotel de Ville, where Robespierre and the other Jacobins were assembled in council. When Henriot brought news of the troops' desertion, Coffinhal, one of the conspirators, cried out, 'It is thy cowardice, villain, that has undone us!' and flung Henriot out of the window. Lébas blew out his brains. The younger Robespierre threw himself from the window, while Couthon, who had sent so many to their deaths, could not steel himself to commit suicide, but crawled beneath the table, where he sat pricking himself with a dagger. Robespierre himself took up a pistol, and putting it to his face, pulled the trigger; but he only succeeded in smashing his lower jaw.

He was still alive when armed men forced their way into the

hall and arrested him with the remaining Jacobins, who were speedily sent to the guillotine. So, with his shattered jaw held in place by a bandage, the 'sea-green incorruptible' laid his neck beneath the knife to which he had sent so many thousands. Within a few hours Marie held in her lap the mutilated head of the man whom her uncle had so often entertained at his table. Did she at that moment call to mind his 'extreme attentiveness' and his 'little acts of courtesy which are expected from a gentleman when sitting next to a lady'?

The death-mask which she made, one of the most striking of her works, can still be seen today in the Chamber of Horrors, not far from those of Marat and Fouquier-Tinville.

The Reign of Terror was over.

CHAPTER SIX

SCOTLAND AND IRELAND

Marie was now thirty-three, and it is inconceivable that her experiences during the past five years had not toughened her character. Even allowing for the fact that she belonged to a less squeamish age than ours, she had witnessed scenes and endured ordeals which would have tested the nerves of the strongest. And in addition to the dangers and anxieties of the Revolution, she had suffered in the previous year a financial blow which would have broken a less resolute woman.

On August 13th, 1793, exactly one month after the murder of Marat, Dr. Curtius died, in circumstances as mysterious as the rest of his life.

'After his death he was opened (the *Memoires* tell us), and a surgical examination took place, when it was fully ascertained that his death had been occasioned by poison.'

Who would poison Dr. Curtius, and why? In an earlier chapter Marie hints at a reason. Curtius had been sent by the Legislative Assembly to the Army of the Rhine when it was commanded by General Custine. This general, in the words of the *Memoirs* 'had committed several errors, through obstinacy and want of judgement, and it was generally supposed that he was the person who caused the poison to be administered.' This mysterious passage suggests that the Doctor may have been sent as a spy—a vocation which is entirely in keeping with what is known of his character.

From every indication in the earlier part of the *Memoirs*, Curtius had been a man of wealth. He acquired pictures and *objéts d'art* and sold them at a profit. His two Exhibitions flourished and brought him in a sizeable income. He always seems to have had money available for the occasional loan or bribe for his Republican friends. Yet after his death Marie discovered to her consternation that he had left debts to the extent of 60,000 francs, for which she became liable.

Why had the Curtius fortune disappeared? We can only guess.

While Curtius had been on the Rhine, Marie had been in prison, and during her absence her mother had been quite unable to cope with the Museum, which was sadly neglected. Now she had to set to work to liquidate the debt. Grimly she began to put the Collection in order and somehow to re-establish the Exhibition, which was her only means of livelihood.

Now it was July, 1794. Robespierre and the leaders of the *Montagne* had been executed. Militarily, the tide had turned and the Revolutionary armies were in triumphant advance. Valenciennes, Landrecis, Le Quesnoy, had fallen successively into their hands. The three Allied armies, Dutch, Austrian and English were separately beaten by the French, and it seemed at last that the country was entering an era of stability and ordered progress. Marie, still young, with vigour, intelligence and talent, took charge of the *Cabinet de Cire*, determined once again to make it a success.

For two years she ran the Exhibition alone, and then, on October 16th, 1795, Marie Grosholtz became Madame Tussaud.

Practically all that is known of François Tussaud is that he was an engineer and came from Mâcon, in Burgundy. He was seven years younger than Marie, and belonged to a family which had been settled in Burgundy for at least 150 years. For several generations the family of Tussaud had been metal-workers, though François, it appears, had been a successful wine-grower before he left Mâcon for Paris.

Until quite recently nothing was known of how and when he met Marie, but Mr. Reginald Edds, of Madame Tussaud's, unearth an interesting fact. He discovered an advertisement, printed in England in 1791 which indicates that in that year, several years before Marie Grosholtz's marriage, D. Curtius had an Exhibition of Waxworks touring England, *under the management of François Tussaud*. It seems likely, therefore, that Marie met her husband when he was her uncle's business associate.

Maybe it was this which gave her the idea of coming to England, but, hampered as she was by the necessity of paying off her uncle's debts, she was forced to remain in Paris for a further seven years. From our point of view, this was fortunate, for it enabled her to watch and record the rise of yet another great contemporary—perhaps the greatest—Napoleon Bonaparte.

The young Corsican artillery officer had begun to be noticed in 1793, during the revolt of the provinces. In that year he had been sent to Toulon with the rank of lieutenant-colonel, to help recapture the town from the rebels and drive out the English and Spaniards, who were helping the royalists. By new methods of artillery attack he had retaken the town and forced the hostile fleets to withdraw. In the following year he had commanded the artillery of the army in Italy, but his ambitions aroused the suspicion of the Government and he had been recalled to Paris. But the following year, 1795, that of Marie's marriage to François Tussaud, gave him the opportunity for which he had been waiting. Once again there was insurrection in Paris. The people rose in arms against the Convention, which expected to be attacked in force by the National Guard. Barras was entrusted with their defence, and he wisely chose as his chief subordinate the recently-disgraced General Napoleon. The story of how Bonaparte, by the skilled use of artillery and the famous 'whiff of grapeshot', put down the rebellion is well known. Says Marie: '. . . No words can convey the intense anxiety and breathless terror with which people waited for the issue of the dreadful conflict; scarcely a family in Paris but had some relative engaged on one side or other of the question. . . . It was half-past four in

the afternoon, when Bonaparte sent eight hundred muskets and
belts to the convention, bidding the members arm, and act as a
corps de reserve, in case of necessity. . . . At length General
Danican, who commanded in chief for the *sections*, began the
attack by a discharge of musketry, to which Bonaparte replied by
such a tremendous hail of grape, that hundreds were brought to
the ground in the Rue St. Honoré. . . . Bonaparte appeared
everywhere, and by the admirable management of his destructive
charges of artillery, he carried victory in every quarter where he
appeared.'

Marie, a soldier's daughter, probably appreciated the military skill of the young Corsican, but did she realize, one wonders, that the days of vast popular insurrections were over, that
civilian mobs with muskets and pikes would never again be a
match for modern artillery handled by a master? Did she recognize that she was watching the rise of the first modern dictator,
a man of the people whose ruthlessness and skill in arms far
exceeded those of the old royalist leaders he had helped to
overthrow?

The victory of the Convention was followed by the formation
of the Directoire, and Bonaparte was made general of a division.
In the following year he married Marie's former fellow prisoner,
Josephine de Beauharnais, and left to command the army in
Italy, where he was again triumphant. Further brilliant victories followed in Austria, and Napoleon was free to carry out
his plans for conquest in the east. Evading Nelson, who was
waiting for him in the Mediterranean, he landed at Aboukir Bay,
defeated the Mamalukes, and having conquered Egypt, marched
into Syria, probably intending an invasion of India in imitation
of Alexander the Great. But at Acre he was halted, and returned
to Egypt, and leaving his army there, sailed for France, arriving
some six weeks later 'dressed [says Marie] in the costume of a
Mamaluke, in large white trousers, red boots, waistcoat richly
embroidered, as also the jacket, which was of crimson velvet.
He arrived about eight in the evening, and the cannons of the
Invalides fired a salute.'

Shortly after his return, the Constitution, which had come into being through the sword, perished by the sword. Napoleon, guarded by his grenadiers, entered the Council of Five Hundred, and in spite of the menaces of its members, dismissed it, as Cromwell had dismissed the House of Commons nearly a century and a half before him. Thus began the Consulate; government by three Consuls, of whom Napoleon himself was the most powerful.

Shortly after this Madame Tussaud was summoned to the Tuileries to take the likeness of Napoleon. She was commanded to be there at six in the morning, and was ushered into a room where, in the words of her *Memoirs* 'she found the renowned warrior with his wife and a Madame Grand-Maison, whose husband was deputy and a partizan of Napoleon's. Josephine greeted her with kindness, conversed much and with extreme affability; Napoleon said little, spoke in short sentences and rather abruptly. When she was about to put the liquid plaster on his face, she begged he would not be alarmed, adding an assurance that it would not hurt him. "Alarmed!" he exclaimed. "I should not be alarmed if you were to surround my head with loaded pistols." Josephine begged Madame Tussaud to be very particular, as her husband had consented to undergo the operation to please her, for whom the portrait was intended.'

By this time, 1801, Madame Tussaud had succeeded in re-establishing the Exhibition in its former popularity, and it is clear that she followed her uncle's practice of carefully cultivating the leading figures of the time. Just as Curtius had modelled the heads of Robespierre, Marat and St. Just, so did Marie display to the delighted Parisian crowds the figures of the Consulate, Napoleon, Lebrun and Cambacères. But by 1802 she had cleared her debt, and, wearied by the bitter experience of thirteen turbulent years, decided to take part of her Exhibition to Great Britain. She was now the mother of two sons, Joseph, born on April 16th, 1798, and Francis, born on August 2nd, 1800.

It may well have been her husband, François Tussaud, who

encouraged her to make this venture; he himself had been in England some years earlier and may have foreseen the commercial possibilities of a touring waxworks show of a type greatly superior to those which the people of Britain had been able to see. For there was nothing new in a waxworks show, and when Marie landed in England she knew she would have to face considerable competition.

So, in May, 1802, Marie landed at Dover with seventy of her exhibits, leaving the balance of her collection with her husband in Paris. She brought with her her eldest son, Joseph, then four years old; little Francis, then only two years of age remained for the time being in Paris.

She had had some difficulty in obtaining permission to leave France, as Fouché, the Minister of Police, whom she knew, at first refused to grant her a passport. 'Fouché was well aware of Madame Tussaud's talents, and therefore opposed her quitting French territory . . . it was contrary to the laws of the country then existing to allow any artists to leave France [but at last] he was prevailed upon to sign Madame Tussaud's passport for England,' probably through the intervention of her friend, Josephine de Beauharnais.

Marie had chosen the right moment to come to England, for only a few months earlier the Treaty of Amiens had established a temporary peace between the two countries. In the following year, 1803, war broke out again and the Channel was closed.

This part of Marie's life is in some ways the most interesting, because it was during her early years in England that she wrote the only letters which have come down to us. Suddenly the discreet, shadowy figure who glides through Hervé's well-padded pages comes to life, and reveals herself as a wife and tender mother. We look over her shoulder as she sits down in her London lodging-house in April, 1803, just before her departure for Edinburgh, to write to her husband, mother and aunt about her troubles, her plans, and her five-year-old son Joseph, whom she calls 'Nini'. She had recently exhibited at the Lyceum Theatre in the Strand.

'MY FRIEND, MY DEAR FRIEND AND MY DEAR FRIENDS— I received your letter with a great deal of pleasure. Nini and I cried with joy and pain at not being able to embrace you. All the same, today is Tuesday and we leave next Tuesday. The Cabinet has been closed since Saturday and all is packed up. M. de Philipstal treats me as you do. He has left me all alone. He is angry. . . .'

M. de Philipstal has already been mentioned in an earlier chapter, when Dr. Curtius got him out of trouble with the Convention by bribing Robespierre. Like Curtius, he was a German and a showman: he exhibited what he called a 'Phantasmagoria', by which he could produce optical illusions, one of which was apparently a 'spectre'. From Marie's letters, it seems that there was a business arrangement between them. M. de Philipstal had lent the Tussauds money and had a financial interest in Marie's exhibition, but the partnership was far from happy. The letter continues:

'M. de Philipstal remains behind until his action with the Baron is finished. He is no longer with the Cabinet. I must go alone and seek fortune. As soon as I arrive in Edinburgh, I will write you and give you my address. I beg you beloved to reply to me at once, as your letters are my only consolation. I will end by embracing you a thousand times. . . . All my love to my dear Françison, mother and aunt and Charlot. Nini is very well and embraces you with all his life and sends you a thousand kisses. I am for life your wife,

TUSSAUD.'

We do not know what was the 'action with the Baron' which kept de Philipstal behind in London, but there is a curious paragraph in a contemporary newspaper which, though it does not mention the showman by name, may be a reference to him.

M. de Philipstal, in one of his advertisements, refers to 'several original astounding and unparalleled experiments in the science of optics . . . which were brought out of his native country [Germany] to do away with the belief of the vulgar in ghosts. . . .' The newspaper paragraph describes how 'Mr. D., a gentleman of fortune of Baker Street, Portman Square, was summoned before a Commissioner of Requests by a foreigner to answer a debt of one guinea which he alleged that Mr. D. owed to him.' Mr. D. (the Baron?) had engaged 'the foreigner' to exhibit, before a select party in his house 'his deception in the spectrological arts'. The report goes on: 'He . . . agreed with the gentleman to entertain the company for the space of one hour for which he was to be remunerated with the sum of one guinea. That accordingly he prepared for his exhibition and had just begun when he was informed by Mr. D. that his exhibition was not agreeable and he need not go on with it. At the same time he presented him with half a guinea which sum he refused to take alleging that Mr. D. was bound by his consent as he was willing to perform his part of it. In answer to the charge Mr. D. acknowledged that he had made the contract and that he did with a view to entertaining some of his friends among whom were a number of young ladies. That on the first appearance of the spectre the ladies were thrown into fits and that it was in consequence of this circumstance that he thought it proper to stop the exhibition. The findings were against Mr. D. who had to pay the guinea.'

Marie's next letter is dated May 11th, 1803, and describes her sea voyage to Scotland:

'MY DEAR FRIEND, MY DEAR FRIENDS, MY DEAR MOTHER AND AUNT—I hope that this will find you all in good health like us. We are all very well. I told you that we left London on the 27th April and arrived in Edinburgh on the 10th May in good health and good company. We had 36 breaks [she refers to the figures] and dozens of confident people were ill through the bad weather. The sea was terribly rough. We saw three storms which lasted three days and everybody had to go below. The boat rolled in a terrifying manner and the Captain who had made this voyage a hundred times had never seen one like it. M. Nini was not afraid. He made friends with the Captain and with everybody. The Captain wished that he had a child like him. He said that he was one of the best sailors and he wanted to train Nini to be a sailor and said he would be a tribute to France. He was well thought of and everybody called him "Little Bonaparte".'

But soon M. de Philipstal crops up again:

'. . . He did not want to give me any money as he said he had paid for the journey. I threatened to return to Paris and when he saw I meant business he gave me £10. One has to be wary of M. Philipstal. . . .'

She goes on to describe her preparations for opening her Exhibition in Edinburgh:

'I have taken a very nice Salon furnished and decorated for £2 a month. I am lodging in the same house with very nice people. The landlady speaks very good French which is lucky for me. Mr. Charles is doubtless going to remain with me for the opening. I hope that the Salon will be ready in a week and that M. Philipstal will be in Edinburgh in a fortnight when his business with the Baron will be finished. . . . We are in a very lovely little town from which we can see the snow-covered mountains. I still have a bad head as though am still on board the boat.

'I have found some compatriots at the Castle and one Lady-in-Waiting who has spent all her life in France. She is very friendly and we spend much time together so that I feel as though I were in Paris which consoles me greatly. M. Nini is dressed like a Prince and spends all day at the Castle playing with a little French boy. My beloved remember me to mother and my Aunt and Francis as their father seeing that their mother is so far away and cannot see him. Nini and I embrace you with all our hearts a thousand times.

I am for life your wife,

TUSSAUD.'

No letters from Françoise Tussaud to his wife have survived, and to judge from her complaint in her next letter he appears to have written very few:

'MY DEAR FRIEND, MY DEAR FRIENDS, MY DEAR FRANÇOIS —I am still waiting to hear from you. This is the hundredth letter which I have written without reply. Why have you not written? I pray you remember I am your wife and that you are the father of my children. If I had Francis with me and my dear mother and aunt as well!'

Perhaps we should not judge François Tussaud too harshly, as at this time war had broken out again between England and France and communications may have been interrupted. Marie goes on to describe the opening of her Exhibition:

'Everybody is amazed at my figures. Nothing like them have previously been seen in this city. . . . It's all very satisfactory for the Salon and I hope to make money in this city. . . . I have asked everybody in this town to look upon Nini as an Englishman and everybody loves him. The town is full of Nini. . . .'

Philipstal had now arrived in Edinburgh, and was again causing trouble:

'I am liked in this town as much as in my own country and not treated as a foreigner. . . . M. Philipstal is very jealous to hear of it. He wants us to mix with no one. He is my enemy and only wishes me harm, but I hope to be done with him in six months time. He is in a bad way and his business is very bad and he has only the Cabinet upon which to rely.'

And she ends with a postscript:

'Give me your news as soon as possible to: Mr. Laurie, Bernard's Rooms, 28, Thistle Street, Edinburgh. If the Channel is closed—write by way of Hamburg.'

Fortunately, copies have survived of the original advertisements for the Exhibition which Madame Tussaud showed to the citizens of Edinburgh in June, 1803. At this stage she had not begun to use her own name, preferring to use that of her uncle, 'the Great Curtius of Paris'. Here is the advertisement in full:

NOW OPEN

At Laurie's, Late Bernards' Room,

Thistle Street

Accurate Models from life in Composition by the

GREAT CURTIUS, OF PARIS

CONSISTS OF: The First Consul, and Madame Bonaparte, Cambacères, Le Brun, Moreau and Kleber. The late Royal Family of France, King, Queen, Princess Royal and Dauphin, M. du Cleri, Valet du Roi, Henry IV of France and Duke of Sully. The late Pope, Mademoiselle Brusse de Perigord who foretold the French Revolution, M. de Voltaire, Jean Jacques Rousseau, Frederick the Great, Mirabeau and the celebrated Dr. Benjamin Franklin of America. Mademoiselle de St. Aramanthe, Mademoiselle de Lassal, Mademoiselle Catlois and Madamoiselle St. Clair—four beautiful young ladies who were guillotined by command of Robespierre. An old Coquette who teased her husband's life out. The beautiful Princess de Lamballe, Madame du Barré—Mistress of Louis XV—who was guillotined. The Count de Lorge who was confined for 20 years in the Bastille, and numberless other celebrated characters besides a great variety of antiquities and interesting curious. . . .

85

In this, one of the earliest of Madame Tussaud's advertisements, only thirty figures are mentioned, and although there were probably more, these were undoubtedly the highlights. In the ensuing years, when the number of figures expanded into hundreds, and when other, more topical personalities took pride of place, this original group—Voltaire, Rousseau, the Comte de Lorge, the Royal Family and the rest—always remained a part of the exhibition; and most of them are still in it to this day. An interesting, somewhat bizarre fact is that the famous 'Sleeping Beauty' whose pneumatic bosom rises and falls to the delight of thousands of children, is the same Madame de St. Aramanthe who was one of the 'four beautiful young ladies guillotined by command of Robespierre'.

To sensitive minds there may be something repulsive in the way in which Marie made a public show of her former friends and enemies, with her 'full-length portrait of Marat in the agonies of death' and her 'accurate model of the guillotine'. But it must be remembered that this was, after all, her only source of livelihood, and if she thought about the matter at all she may have reflected that her friends were now beyond harm and that they might even have approved of the use which she made of them. But we doubt if she ever had such thoughts, for there was steel in Marie's character. We can feel it in her anger with Philipstal, and her disdain for a man she regarded as a charlatan, not fit to be associated with a woman who had walked with kings.

'I can tell you, Sir [she writes to her husband] I think I shall stay in Edinburgh for three months and if all goes well I hope to pay M. Philipstal from the time his share of the expense was started what he has spent—his expenses. . . . Following upon payment he will be without defence. . . . I think I shall be finished with M. Philipstal which will be a good thing and I don't feel in the least disturbed. I have good friends on my side and if he thinks that I am afraid of him he is mistaken. . . . I am taken for a great lady and I have everybody on my side. He has nobody who counts and everyone looks upon M. Philipstal with his Phantasmagoria as a charlatan. In this country the law is on my side.'

Readers may like to know what M. Philipstal had to show the citizens of Edinburgh beside his 'Phantasmagoria'. Here is part of his advertisement in the *Edinburgh Evening Courant* of June 11th, 1803.

'*Two elegant Automatic Figures as large as Nature.* The one representing a Spanish rope dancer six feet high, the other a little boy. Nothing can surpass the admirable construction of these pieces. The large figure seems almost endowed with human faculties—the power of respiration which the mechanism here demonstrates is incredible—he will smoke a pipe and mark the time of the music with a small whistle besides exhibiting the other feats of a rope dances in the exact imitation of life. . . .

'*The self-defending Money Chest.* The mechanism of this piece is ingeniously disposed so that it may with justice be termed the Miser's Life Guardsman—for upon a stranger attempting to force it open by a master key or otherwise, a battery of 4 small pieces of artillery concealed from even the nicest scrutiny will instantly appear and discharge themselves. The very superior excellence of this chest is that the proprietor has always a safeguard against depredations and [it] may with equal advantage be applied to the protection of property in Banking Houses, Counting Houses, Post Chaises, etc. The most adroit in Science declares this to be a masterpiece of mechanism.

'*The Cossack in Miniature.* A small chest in which the little figure representing a Cossack Solo Dancer is contained who opens and shuts the chest when commanded by the audience, appears in a black habit which it throws off with astounding rapidity—presents himself in a handsome gala dress, compliments the Company and dances in the manner of the Cossacks, keeping time accurately with the music.'

On May 18th François Tussaud wrote to Marie, though she did not receive his letter until the first week in June. Her joy and relief at hearing from him overflowed from her letter dated June 9th, a letter from a woman whose love for her husband at this time admits of no doubt:

'MY BELOVED—I received with delight your dear letter of the 18th ultimo. I learnt that all was well with you as indeed it is with my children and all the family, a fact which pleases me and gives me peace of mind. As to myself and our son Nini we are very well, thank God. I like it here very much and quite apart from the people and the very good friends I have found here everything is going well. For example today is the 18th day our waxworks have been opened and we have taken £190 1s. We hope that it will continue like this. Next July we are going to have the fair and horse show which lasts a fortnight. Everybody will come to the Capital from the Provinces and the country and we hope to have a bumper fortnight. . . .'

She then tells François the newest development in her struggle with Philipstal, of her intention to bring an action and dissolve the partnership 'to free myself from his domination which I find insupportable', and mentions that she had had the good fortune 'to become acquainted with the Governor of Edinburgh Castle—a nobleman of high estate'—whose wife had promised Marie her protection. Already the niece of Curtius had begun to follow his habit of cultivating the great.

She is desperate for news of home, and gently chides her husband:

'You have told me, beloved, nothing of what is happening at home, if you have taken a turn at cooking or if you have altered the Salon because I am not ready to return. I am all the same surprised that you have asked me to return without clearing up with Philipstal and at this most critical time when all the ports

88

are closed and communication interrupted between France and Britain.

'I hope to keep my word which I gave you not to return to you until I could bring with me a well-filled purse. It is very fortunate that I made the journey with all our belongings, since the greater part of the heads have been broken and I have had to remake them. I would strongly urge you to take my place at home, to work hard for the children—change the exhibition while I am not there to argue with you. I urge you too, most earnestly to take care of my dear mother, my aunt, my dear Françison and my sister.'

And she ends, pathetically:

'Nini and I join in sending our love with all our heart. Darling remember me. My only joy is to learn all your news and I implore you to see that your letters reach me. If they come by Hamburg send them to someone you know. . . . I repeat, my address is:

> C/o Mr. Laurie,
> Bernard's Room,
> New Town,
> Edinburgh,

Once more adieu, beloved,

> Your wife,
> TUSSAUD.'

What was happening to François Tussaud at this time? Little is known except that he neglected the part of the Exhibition which Marie had left with him and got steadily into debt. A year before Marie left for England they had been forced to mortgage the Exhibition to a certain Salome Reiss. And on April 26th, 1803, Marie had given her husband power of attorney giving him full authority 'to borrow what seems good on the best terms he can, all the money he requires and to compel his said wife to join with him completely in paying the capital and interest laid down in any transaction'. So run the dry legal phrases of the document which the anxious little woman signed in an office at No. 41, Duke Street, Manchester Square, London. All her property inherited from Curtius, the house in the Boulevard du Temple, another house at Ivry were now at her young husband's disposal. No doubt she signed with reluctance, but with the hope that François would not betray her trust in him. Meanwhile she prepared to take her Exhibition from Edinburgh to Glasgow, at her husband's suggestion. In a letter dated July 28th, 1803, she tells him that she has still not been able to break her agreement with Philipstal.

'I have shown our agreement to different lawyers who say there is not the least chance of it being broken legally. The agreement is entirely in his favour. . . . The horse show was held last week. The results were not as favourable as we had hoped —there were very few people there. Philipstal does very little here—he wants to leave next week without telling me definitely where he wants to go. We must, according to your plan, leave here for Glasgow. . . . I am very pleased to learn all at the house are well—as for myself, I am reasonably well for a woman bowed down with anxiety and fear. Nini too is well and learning English quickly and has started to read and take lessons every day. . . .'

And she ends, as usual, by imploring François—

'to look after my dear mother. . . . Nini also sends you his kisses and to his brother Francino. He wants very much to see him. . . . My beloved, I send you my love with all my heart. . . .'

In October the Exhibition opened in Glasgow at the 'New Assembly Hall, Ingram Street'. There were two Salons, the first containing such figures as those of 'the late Royal Family of France . . . Rousseau, Mirabeau, Franklin . . . Bonaparte, Cambacères and Lebrun,' etc., the other exhibiting the heads of the revolutionists 'Robespierre, Fouquier-Tinville, Hebert ...' and 'a full-length portrait of Marat in the agonies of death, after having been assassinated by Charlotte Corday. . . .' The same

Salon also contained a model of the guillotine 'upon a scale of three inches to a foot' and of the Bastille.

Even at this early stage Marie had conceived the idea of separating the famous from the merely infamous, the second Salon being the origin of the Chamber of Horrors, though this name was not given to it until many years later.

In the following year, 1804, she set sail for Ireland. From Waterford on June 20th she writes to her mother and aunt, and, most significantly, not to her husband:

'MY DEAR FRIENDS—I have received your letter dated 7th of June. . . . My son and I are very well indeed . . . have no doubts I shall do very well for the time and I hope to succeed *seeing that I now work only for myself and my children* [our italics]. We endured a very heavy storm at sea but by merciful Providence we are here in Ireland, safe and sound. . . .'

What is not stated in that letter is that she had sailed in convoy (for at that time France was trying to enforce a naval blockade of British shipping), and that the convoy had been scattered by the storm and three ships wrecked within fifteen minutes. One of them was the vessel carrying Madame Tussaud's precious collection, much of which was lost, though some of the figures, having wooden bodies, floated ashore. Marie entered Cork practically penniless, but, undeterred, she set to work to build up her Exhibition again, and within three months was writing about the enthusiastic reception she had been given in Dublin. Marie exhibited in the Shakespeare Gallery, Exchequer Street, where, her advertisement states, are 'to be seen, this and every day, the most beautiful Collection of Figures, executed from life, consisting of Accurate Models in Wax, of the invention of the celebrated Curtius. . . . Figures being elegantly dressed in their proper Costume, are scarcely distinguishable from Life. . . .'

There is a sinister little entry at the foot of this advertisement: 'Ladies and Gentleman may have their Portraits taken in the most perfect imitation of Life; Models are also produced from PERSONS DECEASED, with the most correct appearance of Animation.' Marie certainly had had experience.

It is clear from the last letter that something was happening which lessened Marie's affection for her husband. Since he is imploring her to return, he was obviously not involved with another woman. From what we know of his character in later life, and the fact that even at this period he was in debt, the most plausible inference is that Marie had lost faith in his ability and judgement. In spite of adversity, her enterprise was prospering, whereas from Paris came only news of failure and possibly appeals for money.

Marie began to harden her heart. She saw that her future and that of her children was going to depend more and more on her own talents and initiative. Yet from her previous letters she had clearly been extremely fond of her husband, perhaps even, at one time, in love with him. With no letters from François to guide us, we can only guess at his character. Most probably he was an amiable weakling who appealed at first to Marie's maternal sense and satisfied her desire for children; but that when it became clear that he needed her more than she needed him, she reacted as almost all women do in such circumstances. By losing her respect, he forfeited her love. Later in the same year we find her writing to him:

'They come in crowds every day from six o'clock until ten o'clock. My Cabinet is very well known, since one can see the portraits of the famous and infamous. I leave for Cork, which is a hundred miles to the south. . . . I hope by working hard for my children to give them a good start in life and make them so that their father and mother may be proud of them—this is the wealth we can give them. There will then be no cause for reproach for harm I have done, and I have no regrets. My enterprise is of more importance to me than returning to you. . . . Good-bye, good-bye, we each go our own way. . . .'

Good-bye, good-bye. . . . And yet it was not quite farewell—

yet. For another four years Marie continued to tour her Cabinet under the title of the parent collection in Paris—the Cabinet of Curtius. Her own name never appeared in the advertisements. And her husband, Tussaud had proprietary rights over both the Paris Exhibition, which he had neglected, and its vigorous off-shoot, which Marie was now taking around Great Britain. Until 1808 Marie's intention may have been to make enough money out of her British tour to put both Exhibitions on a sound financial footing, and then return to Paris—in her own good time. But in the spring of that year something happened to make her change her mind, and to make a decision which was to keep her in Britain for the rest of her long life. We can only conjecture that François had done something which finally convinced Marie of his inadequacy. He may have appealed to her for money. We know that he had failed to make the Paris Salon pay, because a few months later Salome Reiss, the mortgagee, foreclosed. In Madame Tussaud's private papers, handed to Mr. Reginald Edds by Mr. Bernard Tussaud, Edds discovered the original notice of foreclosure, written in faded brown ink in Tussaud's own elegant handwriting. The relevant part of the document reads:

'Francois Tussaud cedes to Mademoiselle Salome Reiss all the objects comprising the Salon of figures known as the Cabinet of Curtius. These objects include all the wax figures, all the costumes, all the moulds, all the mirrors, lustres and glass from which she may deem fitting. Mr. Tussaud herewith renounces all rights in this regard. . . .'

Marie never saw her husband again, nor did she ever return to France. She had probably seen the blow coming, for in May, 1808, for the first time since she had taken her Salon to Britain, she dropped the title which had been associated for so long with the Cabinet de Cire in Paris. It is no longer an exhibition of figures 'by the renowned Curtius of Paris'. On May 17th, 1808, readers of the *Belfast News and Letters* saw in its columns the following notice:

MADAME TUSSAUD
Artist
of
The Grand European
CABINET OF FIGURES
Modelled from Life
Which has been Exhibited with great applause
in London and Dublin may now be seen at
No. 92, High Street,
Belfast.

From now on she was alone.

CHAPTER SEVEN

ON THE ROAD

Marie was forty-seven when she finally broke with her husband in 1808. It was the year that Britain came to the aid of Spain in the war against Napoleon, the year of Wellington's ill-starred landing at Corunna. Bonaparte, whose features Madame Tussaud had modelled in the Tuileries seven years previously, was now virtual dictator of Europe. At Austerlitz he had crushed the Russian and Austrian armies, and now he had placed his brother on the throne of Spain. In the following year he divorced Josephine and married the Archduchess Maria of Austria. But his threatened invasion of England had to be abandoned after Nelson's victory at Trafalgar, and though the war was to continue for another seven bitter years the country was no longer in immediate danger. It speaks much for British tolerance that even during these years Marie, who must have been regarded as a Frenchwoman, could continue to tour her Exhibition throughout the British Isles and become ever more popular in the towns she visited.

From 1808 to 1835, a period of twenty-seven years, Madame Tussaud took to the road every year, transporting her figures in caravans, exhibiting in assembly rooms, theatres, inns, town halls, sitting at the cash desk during the day, and working far into the night making fresh models of contemporary personalities to keep her show constantly up to date. And with her went her son Joseph ('Nini') whom, as he grew older, she trained in the craft she had learned from her uncle.

From old handbills and newspapers now lying in the dusty files of museums and public libraries, we can trace her progress.

In June, 1811, the year the Prince Regent came to the throne, she was in Newcastle-on-Tyne. By this time the Cabinet had grown to sixty figures:

MADAME TUSSAUD
Artist

Respectfully informs the nobility and gentry of Newcastle and its vicinity, that the Grand European Cabinet of sixty Figures, which was lately exhibited in Edinburgh with universal approbation, is now open for inspection at the White Hart Inn, Old Flesh Market.

In 1812 Napoleon's Grande Armée was dying in the snows of Russia, Byron had published the first two cantos of *Childe Harold* (and Marie had already modelled the poet) while the Grand European Cabinet of Figures continued its stately progress through the shires. In March it was at Hull 'at No. 4, Market Place'; in July, at York 'in the Dancing Room in Goodramgate, lately occupied by Mr. Goadby'; in October, at Leeds 'in Four Rooms on the Premises lately occupied by Mr. Daniel, opposite the Hotel, Briggate.' Admittance was usually 1s., with 'children under ten years of age, Half-Price'.

This was the period when the Duke of Wellington was the hero of the hour, and when news of his victories over Marshal Soult in Spain began to come through Madame Tussaud immediately modelled his head from an existing bust and put it on show. His great opponent was also being given full prominence. In the winter of 1813, the year of his great triumph at Vittoria, she was in Birmingham, at the Shakespeare Tavern, where, according to a contemporary notice, her collection had recently been enriched 'by the addition of a number of paintings by celebrated artists, among which is a magnificent picture of Bonaparte. . . .'

The year 1815 saw the end of the war with Wellington's final victory and Napoleon's surrender. It would be interesting to know in which town Marie heard the bells pealing for Waterloo, but unfortunately the records are scanty. It is known, how-

ever, that she was at Taunton in March, having arrived there
from Bath. She now proudly announces herself as 'under the
patronage of their Royal Highnesses the Duke and Duchess of
York and Monsieur the Count d'Artois' (brother of Louis XVI,
whom she knew at Versailles). As a royalist, she must have re-
joiced that France was once again a monarchy, though she may
have been amused to reflect that the new King, Louis XVIII,
was the same Monsieur Provence whose face she had been obliged to slap on the stairs at Versailles. . . .

She certainly made good use of him, for four years later, in
1819, one of her catalogues announces on its title-page:

COMPOSITION FIGURES
and other
WORKS OF ART
forming
THE UNRIVALLED EXHIBITION
of
MADAME TUSSAUD
Patronized by his Most Christian Majesty Louis XVIII

We can follow Madame Tussaud's movements fairly closely in
1819. In that year she was in Norwich during January and
February 'at the Large Room, Angel Inn, Market Place'. In
May she visited King's Lynn, moving to Boston in June, where,
'by kind Permission of the Mayor', she was given the use of the
Assembly Room in the Town Hall. At Lincoln, in July, she
again uses the Assembly Rooms; in August she goes to Newark,
and at Nottingham, where she stayed for nearly two months her
'Ninety Public Characters' were shown 'in the large Room at the
Exchange'. She ended the year by visiting Derby ('the Old
Assembly Room') in November, and Sheffield in December. By
this time the list of royal and noble patrons had grown to five.
In addition to Louis XVIII, the Count d'Artois and the Duke
and Duchess of York, her advertisement gives as patrons, '. . .
the late Royal Family of France', and 'her Grace the Duchess of
Wellington'.

An interesting point to note is that Marie's Exhibition had now achieved such prestige that it was nearly always opened by 'His Worship the Mayor'. From her Press announcements and catalogues it is very clear that she wanted to dissociate herself from the general run of waxwork exhibitions, of which there were hundreds. She even gives up the use of the word 'wax', preferring 'composition'. For instance, her announcement to the people of Derby in 1819 states: 'Madame Tussaud hopes that the Ladies and Gentlemen will not form any opinion from them, that her Exhibition is different from any collection that has ever been shown in this or any other kingdom, it being entirely a composition of her own invention, and which every visitor from actual observation may judge is very superior to any figures in wax that can possibly be made, being entirely devoid of that disagreeable hue which wax figures invariably possess, and which has naturally prejudiced many persons against this kind of exhibition. . . .' What some of the rival Exhibitions were like can be gathered from a Press notice dated September 24th, 1819, in a Nottingham newspaper: 'We have now had an opportunity of viewing Madame Tussaud's elegant exhibition of Composition Figures and dare assert without fear of contradiction, that it far exceeds anything of the kind ever seen before in this town. Instead of a number of unmeaning sallow faces, sitting in rows behind benches covered with green cloth . . . the room presents the scene of the utmost gaiety. We were astonished on entering it to behold a vast number of full-length figures standing, sitting and lying, in splendid attire, the whole bearing the appearances of real life. Indeed, a stranger must be some time in the room before he can ascertain which are the figures and which the spectators. . . .' Incidentally, a Lincoln newspaper of this year contains the first recorded instance of the well-known Tussaud story about the spectator, who addresses one of the figures by mistake, imagining it to be human. 'The inimitable figure of the artist is an excellent deception, and being placed at the entrance of the rooms, has caused many ludicrous mistakes: in one instance a person of this city *twice* addressed himself to it, and receiving no answer, turned away highly chagrined at the supposed rudeness of Madame.'

At this point let us look at her Catalogue of Exhibits and see how the Salon has developed since it was first shown at the Lyceum Theatre, London, in 1802, and at Edinburgh in 1803. Our copy bears the signature of its original owner, a 'Mrs. Coombe', with the date 'February 15th, 1819'.

Printed by A. and J. Goode, of Bridge Street, Cambridge, its title is:

Biographical and Descriptive
SKETCHES
of the whole-length
COMPOSITION FIGURES
and other
WORKS OF ART
forming
THE UNRIVALLED EXHIBITION
of
MADAME TUSSAUD

Inside the title-page there is a discreet little notice stating that 'The following pages contain a general outline of the history of each character represented in the Exhibition; which will not only greatly increase the pleasure to be derived from a mere view of the Figures, but will also convey to the minds of young Persons, much biographical knowledge—a branch of education universally allowed to be of the highest importance.' Madame always recognized that children were among her best customers.

Then follows a series of biographical sketches of the characters represented, each with a number corresponding with that on a card fixed to the figure.

There are ninety figures in all, beginning with George III ('Taken from Life, in 1809') and ending with Robespierre ('Taken from his head after Execution'). The biography of

George III ends on a fine peroration: 'The reign of His Majesty has been longer in duration than that of any of his predecessors. It has been productive of events of the highest importance to posterity. . . . The American War—the French Revolution—the career of Bonaparte—and the restoration of the Bourbons to the Throne of France—are events that have shaken Europe to her centre. But amidst the general and desolating shock, England! happy England! defended, under Providence, by the virtues of her monarch, her courage and her wisdom, has weathered the storm, and enfolded in the arms of victory and prosperity, her matin and her evensong are still the same—GOD SAVE THE KING!' The Prince Regent fares almost as well: 'He has filled the dignified station of Regent in a manner that has endeared him to those subjects over whom, in all probability, Heaven has destined him to reign as Monarch; and the best that we can wish him is, that he may become as good a King as he has been a Regent. He then cannot fail to preserve what he now possesses—the love and respect of a free and happy people.' It is hard to realize that this was the same man who, two years before, had been stoned by the people as he drove through London to open Parliament.

Near by stand the Princess of Wales, Princess Charlotte of Wales, the Prince of Saxe-Coburg and the Duke and Duchess of York, all, in the words of the Catalogue 'Taken from Life'. This, of course, was the 'Grand old Duke of York'—

> Who had ten thousand men;
> He marched them up to the top of the hill
> And he marched them down again.

according to an unkind contemporary ballad. Marie contents herself with saying that 'At the commencement of the later war of 1792, his Royal Highness, who for some time commanded the British forces on the Continent, displayed great personal valour.'

Other Royal personages on view are Queen Elizabeth ('her affection for the Earls of Leicester and Essex showed that she

was not proof against the attacks of the urchin God of Love'),
Mary, Queen of Scots, and 'Charles Stuart, the Pretender'.

The Duke of Wellington comes next, and here the biographer
excels himself: 'For the character of this great man, despairing
of doing justice to it, we, like the painter of antiquity, draw over
it a veil. Who is there that knows not of Wellington? Lives
there a man who has not heard of Waterloo?'

Literature is represented by Shakespeare, the drama by
Kemble 'in the character of Coriolanus' and Mrs. Siddons
as Queen Katherine. Marie modelled the head of Shakespeare
from the Droushout bust of Stratford-on-Avon Church;
Kemble was modelled 'from Life, in 1800' (presumably during
a visit to Paris, or had Marie made a mistake in her date?), while
the divine Sarah was 'taken from a Bust executed in 1804'.
There are also figures of William Pitt, Charles James Fox, John
Knox 'from a Picture, in Holyrood House, Edinburgh' (a relic
of Marie's Scottish visits), John Wesley and 'The Right Hon. H.
Grattan . . . the celebrated orator', included, perhaps, because
he had 'Always been a strenuous advocate for the claims of the
Irish Catholics, by whom he is looked up to as a champion'.

The head of Napoleon is stated to have been 'Taken when he
was on board the *Bellerophon*, off Torbay, in 1815'. If this is
true, it is a pity that no record exists of the meeting which must
have been a strange one. One wonders if the fallen giant remembered in Madame Tussaud his former wife's young friend,
who came to the Tuileries in 1801, and to whom he said,
'Madame, I should not be alarmed if you surrounded my head
with loaded pistols.' The biographical note ends: 'A prisoner
on the rock of St. Helena, he presents a melancholy spectacle of
human greatness. He who once could make the mightiest
monarchs tremble at his frown, at last is himself become an object of pity. But amidst all his misfortunes, the motto of
Napoleon appears to be *Dum spiro, spero*.'

All the older figures which Madame Tussaud brought with
her from Paris are still on view, Louis XVI and 'The Late
Queen of France', the Dauphin, Madame Elizabeth (oddly, the

biographical note does not mention her friendship with Madame Tussaud), the Duchess of Angoulême and the Princess de Lamballe, of whom the Catalogue says: 'The murderers carried the bleeding head to Madame Tussaud, the Artiste, and obliged her to take a model of it, which dreadful order she, more dead than alive, dared not refuse to obey.'

One of the most curious exhibits, which still survives in the modern exhibition, is the head of an old woman of unexampled hideousness, described in the Catalogue as 'A Coquette—taken from life'. It appears to be Marie's only attempt at caricature, and in order that his readers shall be in no danger of missing the point, the writer of the biographical note has italicised all the words referring to the lady's alleged charms. It reads: 'The name of this *elegant* and *beautiful* woman was Madame Sappé. She was the wife of a rich merchant at Paris. She had a happy knack of *conversation*. "Oh! ye Gods, how she would talk." But the cruel guillotine took off the head of this lovely creature. We have heard of young men becoming enamoured of a statue; we caution young gentlemen to beware that the same does not happen to them, while gazing on the *charms* of the *interesting* Madame Sappé.' One is left wondering what Madame Sappé had done to Madame Tussaud. . . .

At the far end of the hall and not, at this time separated from the rest, are the leaders of the Revolution and some of its grim relics. The Comte de Lorge ('Madame Tussaud is a living witness of his being taken out of that prison on the 14th July, 1789'), Robespierre ('. . . he rendered up his bloodstained soul on the guillotine, at the age of 35, a poor sacrifice at the altar of justice and outraged nature'), and models of the Bastille and the guillotine.

It was the latter model which, later that year, gave to a young man of Lincoln the idea of making a copy, with a result which was reported in a Lincoln newspaper on July 30th, 1819: 'Last week a young man of this city, upon examining the model of the French guillotine in Madame Tussaud's collection, wished practically to prove the power of this fatal instrument, and caused one to be made on a small scale for the purpose of cutting off the heads of fowls, etc. On Thursday an experiment was made upon a couple of ducks. A youth servant in the house, was executioner, but not being very dexterous in his office, he had the forefinger of his left hand cut off.'

To complete the Exhibition there is a self-portrait of Madame, and, with an apologetic note, studies of her two sons. 'It may naturally be supposed,' says the Catalogue, 'that she would model those persons to whom she is connected by the ties of nature and affection, and as she flatters herself that the likenesses are good, she trusts that the placing of them in the Exhibition may be pardoned.' The Catalogue ends with a note stating that: 'J. P. Tussaud, son of Madame Tussaud, respectfully informs the Nobility, Gentry and the Public in General that he has a Machine, by which he takes Profile Likenesses with the utmost accuracy. Price 2s. to 3s. according to style.'

In the following year, 1820, George III died and the Prince Regent became George IV. It was the year in which his disowned Queen, Caroline of Brunswick, whom he had neglected and maltreated, tried to force her way into the Abbey during the Coronation Ceremony. There was considerable popular anger against the King; nevertheless the people of Britain, particularly those in the provinces, eagerly read every scrap of news relating to the Coronation. In our own time this curiosity would have been amply satisfied by Press, radio, TV and films. In 1820 the travelling waxworks show provided the only means by which most English people could share by proxy in the pageantry of Westminster. Marie was not a woman to miss such a chance, and she grabbed it with both hands. For several years afterwards her Coronation Tableau was one of the main attractions of the Exhibition. At Wakefield, in April, her advertisement mentions 'His Present Majesty George IV' and 'Her Majesty Queen Caroline', though these were probably the existing figures as shown in the previous year. But soon her Coronation Group was ready, and a catalogue dated 1822 begins:

FIRST GROUP
in
THE CENTRE OF THE ROOM
represents the
CORONATION OF HIS MOST GRACIOUS MAJESTY
GEORGE IV

wearing the Imperial Crown, with the Sceptre in his hand—He is dressed in his magnificent crimson velvet Robes of State, as worn by him on that august occasion; supported on his right hand by the Duke of York; in his Robes of State; and by his Grace the Archbishop of Canterbury on his left—The figure of His Royal Highness Prince Coburg, in his beautiful Robes of the Order of the Garter; and his Grace the Duke of Wellington, in his Robes of State—Also, a figure of the Champion, in a suit of real armour; and three beautiful allegorical figures, representing Britannia, Hibernia, and Caledonia.

The figure of the unfortunate Queen Caroline had been quietly dropped from the Exhibition. She had died in the previous year.

An interesting point about this 1822 catalogue is that the heads of the Revolutionists are now exhibited in a separate room. It has been suggested that this was done at the suggestion of a don when Madame Tussaud exhibited her figures at Cambridge, though many years before Marie had already tried the experiment. The second part of the Catalogue begins:

The following
Highly Interesting
FIGURES AND OBJECTS
in consequence of the
PECULIARITY OF THEIR APPEARANCE
are placed
IN AN ADJOINING ROOM
and form
A SEPARATE EXHIBITION
well worthy of the inspection of Artists and Amateurs
Madame charges visitors to this room an extra 6d.

The exhibits included the figures of Marat, 'one of the most atrocious leaders of the French Revolution . . . delighting in blood', Carrier, Fouquier-Tinville, Hebert and the unfortunate Count de Lorge. There was also a model of the guillotine, and the shirt of Henry IV 'when stabbed by Ravaillac . . . the stain of the blood which issued from the wound can still be seen on it. . . . When Madame Tussaud was in Edinburgh His Highness' (the Count d'Artois) 'wished to purchase the shirt for 200 guineas, but she declined parting with an article of such great curiosity.'

Madame knew well that such an object, together with her relics of the Revolution, would draw gate-money far in excess of the Count's 200 guineas. She had had ample experience of the public appetite for horrors. She had suffered by it, and now she began to make use of it. From this time onwards her 'Separate Exhibition' became an increasingly important feature of her show; a recognition that the infamous had an even greater box-office value than the famous.

During the winter of 1824–5 Marie toured the Eastern Counties, visiting Cambridge in October and November, 1824, where she opened in the Town Hall 'by permission of the Right Worshipful the Vice-Chancellor, and the Worshipful the Mayor and Magistrates'. In her advertisement she points proudly to the fact that her Exhibition had been patronized by the University of Oxford. In January she was at Colchester, in Essex, at the Assembly Rooms attached to the Three Cups Inn.

Year after year Marie's caravans rumbled along the dusty roads of a Britain which was changing before her eyes. She visited the growing industrial towns again and again; Stockton, Durham, Sunderland, Sheffield, Leicester and others. She travelled over roads newly improved by Macadam and Telford, roads on which a mail coach could run at the unheard-of speed of eight miles an hour. She heard the hum of the looms in Manchester and Preston, saw the huddled houses of the mill-hands spreading out over the fellsides; read, in 1829, that a Mr. George Stephenson had produced a railway locomotive—the 'Rocket'—

which had so impressed the directors of the Liverpool and Manchester Railway Company that they had decided to use locomotives instead of stationary engines pulling a cable. And she saw the older England too, the gracious squares and crescents of Bath, the domes and spires of Oxford. She knew this country in all its moods and seasons, the blossoming orchards of the Severn Valley in spring; the wooded hills of Shropshire in June; the wet streets of Manchester in December.

As an artist, she must have been particularly conscious of the change in clothes. The fashionable dress of the seventeen-seventies—powdered wigs and silk knee-breeches of the men, the widespreading skirts and high-piled head-dresses of the women had vanished with the world of her girlhood. So had the Empire style which followed, and now men wore their own hair and sported wide-brimmed top-hats, high cravats, long tight-fitting trousers and short, tight jackets: while the women's skirts fell in loose folds from a waistline which had risen to just below their breasts. All around her she saw change, and as one by one her old friends and enemies died she must at times have felt like a survivor from another age.

In 1826 her mother, whom she had not seen for twenty-five years, had died. Since the failure of François Tussaud, Madame Grossholtz had taken charge of Marie's younger son, Francis, but after the death of his grandmother the young man, now aged twenty-six, joined his mother and brother in England. He too was a skilful modeller.

Madame Tussaud was now sixty-five, and though she remained in control of her Exhibition much of the work of running it devolved upon her two sons, though she never ceased to make additions to her collection. While visiting Edinburgh in 1828, she took the opportunity of modelling the heads of the notorious body-snatchers, Burke and Hare. At the same time, balancing the famous with the infamous, she made a portrait bust of Sir Walter Scott.

In 1830, the year George IV ended his short reign, she was in the Midlands again, visiting Leicester, Stafford and Shrewsbury. Besides Burke and Hare, Lord Byron and Sir Walter Scott had now joined the collection. So had Marie's former patron, the Count d'Artois, who, having returned to France from Britain had again been driven into exile in that year. From this period also dates one of Madame Tussaud's most illuminating posters, issued in Portsmouth, and worth quoting because it reveals a frank acceptance of class divisions which are hardly conceivable in Britain today. The poster reads:

Madame Tussaud and Sons return their thanks for the support their Exhibition has met with, and they respectfully announce, that it must **finally close in a few days.** At the same time considering that a large class of persons are unavoidably excluded from viewing the Collection, in consequence of the pressure of the time, they have made arrangements to admit

THE WORKING CLASS
During the time the Exhibition remains
for Half Price,

from a **Quarter before Nine till Ten** in the Evening. By this arrangement, sufficient time will be given for both classes to view the collection without interfering with each other, and they hope that none but those so situated will take advantage of it, as, if known, they will be refused.

The last sentence can only mean that if the nobility and gentry try to get in at half-price by wearing navvy's breeches, and Madame spots them, there is going to be trouble.

When William IV came to the throne in 1830 Marie was nearly sixty-nine, but her hands had lost nothing of their skill, for in that year she set to work to make yet another Coronation Group, though she retained some of the figures from the previous one, including the three allegorical figures representing Britannia, Caledonia and Hibernia. At this period her son Joseph, who was thirty-two, was also doing a considerable share of the modelling.

The newspapers continued to give high praise. 'When we consider,' says the *Leicester Journal* for January 8th, 1830, 'that

107

this immense Collection is subject to frequent removals, it is really astonishing that it can be done without injuring the figures; add to this the small charge demanded for admission, it is surprising that so small a sum can pay the numerous expenses with which it is attended.' In a later issue of the same journal the Exhibition is described as 'the grandest collection of Waxworks ever exhibited in this Town'.

The exhibition was held in 'The Theatre, Leicester, which is fitted up to represent a Splendid Saloon, 70 feet in length' Madame Tussaud usually hired the local theatre when she could not obtain a room of sufficient size to house her now greatly enlarged collection. She can also claim to have invented the Promenade Concert. Nearly always a band was engaged to play during the evening, and on certain occasions Madame herself performed 'on the pianoforte'. During the exhibition at Leicester, for instance, the *Leicester Journal* notes that 'the Promenade every evening presents a very lively appearance, heightened by the performance of a Quadrille Band, stationed in the Gallery'.

It is tempting to look back on the thirties of the last century as a time of tranquillity and peace; to imagine Madame and her Exhibition moving through a Britain of Dickensian inns, jolly, red-faced farmers and endearing old country gentlewomen. It is a pleasant but misleading picture. There was much unrest both in the country and in the towns.

Parliamentary reform was the question of the hour. The continuing shift of population from the country to the towns had brought about serious electoral anomalies. The 'rotten boroughs', places like Old Sarum and Bramber—barely discoverable on the map—still returned representatives to Parliament, while great industrial centres like Manchester, Birmingham and Bristol had no independent representation at all. Cobbett, Jeremy Bentham, John Stuart Mill, Hume and Francis Place were, in a sense, the Voltaires and Rousseaus of the age; they expressed in polished phrase and noble oratory the grievances of the inarticulate masses. In 1831, Earl Grey's Whig Ministry presented a Bill to Parliament which disenfranchised sixty boroughs, and deprived forty-seven others of one member each, while it gave members to counties or large towns hitherto unrepresented. At the Second Reading the Bill passed by a majority of only one, so the Government went to the country and were returned with a majority of 100. Again the Bill was presented and passed by a majority of 136. Then the House of Lords threw it out.

A wave of anger swept the country. At Birmingham 150,000 people passed a resolution refusing to pay taxes unless the Bill was passed. At Nottingham the people burnt down the castle. In the West Country reformist leaders who had protested were put under arrest, and in October a Special Commission arrived in Bristol to try them. It was headed by the Recorder, a certain Judge Wetherall, who was heartily hated by West Country folk.

On the morning of October 29th the Recorder arrived in the city. Knowing the mood of the people and fearing a disturbance, the authorities swore in a number of special constables, who did more harm than good. Their officiousness angered the crowd and throughout the day there were ugly scenes. That night Judge Wetherall banqueted with the Corporation, while in the streets outside crowds were gathering, shouting and demonstrating. Not far away, in a house in Queen's Square, a little group of people listened anxiously to that murmuring mob. To one of them the noise was only too familiar, though it was now more than forty years since she had last heard it. Madame Tussaud, with her two sons, were in Bristol with their Exhibition. She was nearing her seventieth birthday.

That night the mob attacked the Mansion House. The civic banquet broke up in confusion, Wetherall and his hosts escaping over the roof tops. Suddenly the cry rose, 'To the back!' The mob surged into the offices behind the Mansion House, where firewood was stored, but for the time being did not set fire to the building, but looted it thoroughly. They broke into the cellars, brought out a hundred dozen of wine, and were soon too drunk to be capable of further mischief.

109

Then followed three days and nights of terror. In the morning the rioters assembled in Queen's Square, watched by Madame and her sons. One man climbed on to the statue of King William and waved a tricoloured cap on a pole. 'Behold the Cap of Liberty!' he shouted. This aroused in the minds of the rioters a vague memory of the French Revolution, when the people of Paris had stormed the Bastille. Bristol's Bastille was its gaol, to which the crowd now hurried, carrying sledge-hammers with which they broke open the doors and liberated the prisoners. Then they broke in the Governor's House, pitched his books into the river, then set fire to the house. Drunk with success, and knowing that the authorities were helpless against them, they visited the Bishop's Palace, the lock-up house at Lawford's Grate, and the Gloucester County Gaol, leaving them all in flames.

At eight o'clock that night Madame Tussaud watched them as they poured back into Queen's Square. She could see some wandering about the rooms of the deserted building with lighted candles while others again plundered the cellars, and began rolling out barrels of wine and beer. Suddenly flames leaped from the curtained windows; the mob cheered, and within two hours the whole great building was ablaze.

Did Marie, as she heard the crackling of the flames and watched the firelit faces of the rioters, remember that night when she saw the flames of the burning barracks of Tuileries lighting the sky, while her brothers and cousins went down fighting for the doomed monarchy of France?

Later the rioters chalked on the door of the house which contained her Exhibition a cross, marking it for destruction. Other houses in the Square were already on fire. Boys in their 'teens made a house-to-house visitation, giving the householders half an hour's notice to leave before they set fire to their homes. Most seemed to have accepted the situation apathetically, but not Madame Tussaud. The old lady told her sons to clear the building as quickly as possible, and pile the figures outside. Meanwhile a 'stalwart and loyal Negro', a servant of Madame, placed himself at the door and kept the crowd at bay with a blunderbuss.

It was now Monday night, and the riots had continued for three days. Outside, piled on the pavement, lit by the glare of the flames, were some of Madame's precious figures; but whether from fear of the blunderbuss or, perhaps, admiration of Madame's pluck, the rioters did not touch them. And by an odd trick of Fate, a young artist, William Muller, was at that moment making a picture of the scene, and in his drawing, which survives today, we can see quite clearly the house in which Madame Tussaud housed her Exhibition, and the wax figures lying outside it. Then at eight o'clock she turned to her sons with joy and relief in her eyes. Above the drunken shouts of the mob she heard the drums and fifes of the 11th Infantry Regiment. The mob began to disperse. The soldiers marched in. The riots were at an end.

CHAPTER EIGHT

THE FAMOUS AND THE INFAMOUS

After 1831 Madame Tussaud continued to tour her Exhibition for a few more years. We know that she revisited Oxford and Reading from April to July, 1832, and that in the following year she spent four months in Brighton, then moved on to Canterbury, Dover, Maidstone and Rochester. At the end of the year her Exhibition was housed in the Assembly Rooms attached to the Green Man Hotel at Blackheath. Among the figures were those of Burke and Hare and 'Denis Collins (taken from life at the gaol, Reading) in the identical dress he had on when he made the atrocious attempt on His Majesty's Life at Ascot Heath Races', proving that Madame still had an eye for any likely malefactor who would grace her 'Separate Room'. She was now moving ever nearer London, and I believe that, after her experiences in Bristol, Marie had for some time been thinking of giving up her tours and bringing her caravans to rest in the capital. She was now an old lady of seventy-two; both her sons were married, and she may well have thought that the time had come to rest from wandering. She had achieved the task she had set herself in 1804, when she wrote to her husband: 'I hope by working hard for my children to give them a good start in life and make them so that their mother and father may be proud of them—this is the wealth we can give them.'

Blackheath was the last town to see Madame Tussaud's Exhibition before it moved finally to London. On Boxing Day, 1833, Londoners saw a placard which read:

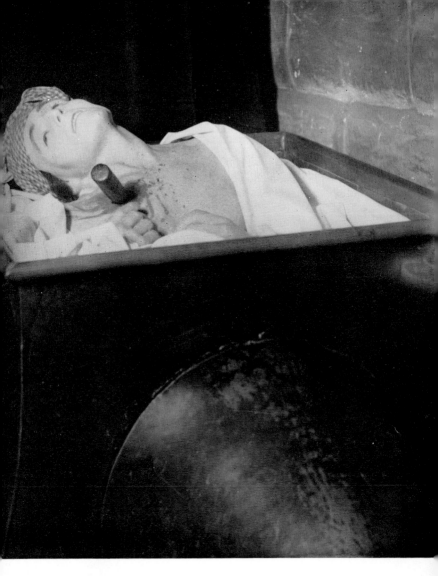

*Jean-Paul Marat modelled, as he lay dead in his bath,
by Madame Tussaud*

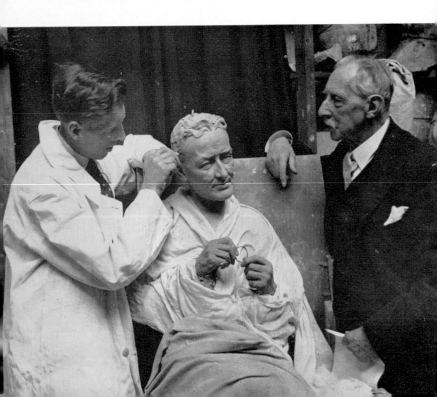

LEFT *John Reginald Halliday*
Christie. Executed on the 15th July
1953, at Pentonville for the murde[r]
of his wife
BELOW *Bernard Tussaud and h[is]*
father John T. Tussaud working on [a]
model of William Wilberforce in 19[

ROYAL LONDON BAZAAR
GRAY'S INN ROAD
(Which has been fitted up for the purpose)
Carriages may wait in the Arena.
Lately arrived from the Town Hall, Brighton,
and last from the Assembly Rooms, Green Man, Blackheath.
SPLENDID NOVELTY
Coronation Groups and Musical Promenade
ENTIRELY NEW
MADAME TUSSAUD AND SONS

followed by a detailed description of the exhibits.

During the following year Madame Tussaud exhibited in Camberwell, in Hackney, and in the Strand before she found a suitable home for her Exhibition. It was a large, shed-like building in Baker Street called the Portman Rooms, and had once been a Mess Hall for the Brigade of Guards. On March 24th, 1835, Madame Tussaud's Exhibition opened its doors to Londoners for the first time in its new permanent home, where it remained for forty-nine years until its removal to a building on the present site.

As a girl Marie had known the France of the *Grands Seigneurs* and watched the Revolution which destroyed it. As a woman she had seen the rise and fall of Napoleon, had lived under the Regency and under three British Kings. Now, for the remainder of her long life she was to see the beginning of yet another era, that of Victoria. For two years after Madame Tussaud moved to Baker Street, William IV died, and Victoria, then a girl of eighteen, began her reign.

We have before us as we write a series of Exhibition catalogues, published after Madame moved to London. The first is dated 1834, and from that year we can trace the evolution of the Exhibition as, year by year, Marie and her two sons improved and added to it. At first it is very similar to her touring show. The 1834 Catalogue begins with the usual Coronation of William IV, and is followed by Lord Brougham, the Lord

Chancellor; the Duke of Wellington; and Earl Grey, Premier of England. The earlier monarchs George IV, George III, are still there, but they have had to move farther back in the queue. Literature is represented by Shakespeare, Scott and Byron, with Kemble and Mrs. Siddons still holding the fore for drama, and Swedenborg for philosophy. But in the 'Separate Room' the 'old faithfuls', Marat, Fouquier-Tinville, and the rest, have one or two new companions: the death-mask of Corder, 'murderer of the unfortunate Maria Martin', and Holloway, the 'atrocious wretch who murdered his wife in a manner too horrible to describe'. This is saying much, for Marie's catalogue-writer did not spare his readers, and his zestful description of the tortures inflicted on Ravaillac, the assassinator of Henry IV, proves that our ancestors had strong stomachs.

In 1838 William IV has become 'His late Majesty' and there is now a group representing 'Her Most Gracious Majesty Victoria and her august mother, the Duchess of Kent'. Of Victoria the Catalogue notes briefly: 'Her Majesty, to a prepossessing exterior, is understood to add those qualities calculated to endear her to her country, and to place her in that enviable situation in the hearts of a free people, which must make her the envy and the admiration of the world.'

Farther down the room, Cromwell now stands beside Queen Elizabeth; and Sir Robert Peel, Lord Melbourne, Hume and Cobbett are other additions to the gallery of the famous.

The 'Separate Room' for the infamous boasts a new murderer, James Greenacre, who 'barbarously murdered and mutilated Hannah Brown, whose remains he dispersed in various parts of the Metropolis'. He had been executed in the previous year, and the model must have been one of the current attractions to visitors in 1838.

Two years later, the Catalogue for 1840 includes the 'Coronation of Her Most Gracious Majesty Queen Victoria' and 'The Unfortunate Mary, Queen of Scots, reproved by John Knox'. Madame had always had a warm place in her heart for Scotland, and throughout most of the time her Exhibition was on tour the

Queen of Scots usually had a place in it. As the years passed Madame Tussaud and her sons developed bigger and more ambitious groups; they were no longer restricted by room and could give their imaginations full play. At this time it is unlikely that Madame herself was responsible for the bulk of the new figures; she probably reserved for herself only subjects which had a personal appeal for her. Now the arts begin to get a bigger showing. Kemble and Mrs. Siddons are joined by 'Mr. Liston in the character of Paul Pry'. Liston, a forgotten Victorian actor, is described in the 1840 Catalogue as '. . . the incomparable professor of the mimic art . . . too universally known, and his talents justly admired, as to render detail necessary; we cannot omit, however, that the season he performed the character in which he is here represented, he brought into the Haymarket exchequer the enormous sum of £7,000'.

Music is now represented by Paganini, who had died in that year, and by a singer, Madame Malibran de Beriot. And there are two new murderers, Courvoisier 'the horrid murderer of the helpless Lord William Russell', and Richard Gould, 'now on his way to the penal settlements'; and a murderee, 'Eliza Davis, who was killed in Frederick Street, near Regent's Park', not far from the Exhibition.

Two years later Joseph Tussaud, Madame's elder son, made a remarkable discovery. John Theodore Tussaud, his great-grandson, tells the story in his book, *The Romance of Madame Tussaud's*: 'Mr. Joseph Tussaud, the elder son of Madame Tussaud, was a great lover of London, and it was his delight to roam leisurely about the Metropolis, studying the streets and byways and the people who traversed them.

'In one of these peregrinations during the spring of 1842 he found himself leaning over the parapet of London Bridge, watching the movements of the diversified craft on the river, when he observed by the wharves of Billingsgate a carriage being hoisted ashore from the deck of a ship like a huge spider hanging from its web.

'That in itself was probably a fairly frequent occurrence, and it would have passed from Mr. Tussaud's memory except for what followed. There were numbers of people looking over the bridge—as may be seen today, and will be seen for many a day to come—and my great-uncle suddenly heard the voice of a countryman next to him saying, "That's a very fine carriage, but I know where there's a finer that some people would give a lot to have. I could take you to a place where you could see the self-same carriage in which Napoleon tried to escape from Waterloo." '

The man was right. He led Tussaud, the one man in London to whom it mattered most, to a repository in Gray's Inn Road, where he found the historic coach in the possession of a Mr. Robert Jeffreys, who had taken it in part payment of a bad debt. Previously it had been in the possession of a travelling showman named William Bullock, from whom it had passed to Jeffreys, a coachbuilder. Joseph Tussaud bought the coach, which for eighty-three years was one of the leading attractions of the Exhibition until it was destroyed in the fire of 1925.

The coach, with other relics of Napoleon, is described in a catalogue dated 1845. By this time, ten years after the Exhibition had moved into the Portman Rooms, it had expanded greatly. One hundred and ninety figures are mentioned in the Catalogue, and for the first time we find the title 'The Chamber of Horrors' applied to the 'Separate Room', for admission to which Madame charged an extra 6d. A contributor to Punch was responsible for the change. He had so described the room in an article, intending it as a joke, but the name stuck, and soon it was adopted officially. A regular visitor to the Exhibition was the Duke of Wellington, who asked to be kept informed of any additions to the collection. His favourite figures were those of Queen Victoria and the dead Napoleon, but he also enjoyed the Chamber of Horrors. When Joseph Tussaud expressed surprise to this, the 'Iron Duke' replied sharply: 'Well, they represent *fact*, don't they?' There were also two additional rooms devoted entirely to Napoleonic relics. The first is described in the 1842 Catalogue as:

116

SMALL ROOM, OR GOLDEN CHAMBER
Madame Tussaud and her sons' New Rooms
of
RELICS OF THE EMPEROR NAPOLEON
Admission to the Shrine, Sixpence

A long preamble describes how the relics had been acquired at a cost of £5,000 and states rather ingenuously that 'they are such as ought not to be, with propriety, in private hands; but should take their place in the Invalides' in Paris . . . and as all those that originally were Prince Lucien's [Napoleon's brother] are affirmed before Masters in Chancery, and were intended by him to have been the property of his son, the King of Rome, but never reached him, and were sent to the prince on the death of his mother . . . there can be no doubt of their authenticity.'

The detailed list of relics, amounting to 151, provides a curious commentary on the fascination which the dead dictator still exercised over the minds of the public. Would British people today pay 6*d*. to visit the 'Shrine' of Adolf Hitler? Yet from 1842 onwards thousands paid their sixpences to pore over Napoleon's 'Celebrated Camp Bed, used by the Emperor during 7 years at St. Helena, with the original Mattresses and Pillow on which he died', his gold repeating watch, his tooth-brush, his table knife, his pair of shoe-socks, his 'Shirt, Under Waistcoats, Drawers, and Madras Handkerchief' and even a 'Tooth of Napoleon, extracted by Dr. O'Meara' and 'the instrument used by Dr. O'Meara to draw Napoleon's teeth'. One is distressed to read in the Catalogue that 'the Emperor suffered much' during this operation.

In an adjoining room stood the Waterloo carriage with its built-in writing-desk, secret jewel-compartment, gun-rack and special compartment for pistols 'ready at hand in case of emergency'. The coach and all the Napoleonic relics were destroyed in the great fire of 1925. Only the charred and blackened axle now remains.

Besides adding to the collection of contemporary and near-contemporary figures Madame Tussaud and Sons were now building up an Historical Group. The 1845 Catalogue describes figures of Charles I, Charles II, James II, William III, Cardinal Wolsey and Joan of Arc, in addition to those of Cromwell and Queen Elizabeth shown in previous years. Great care was taken over the details of the costumes, 'the whole faithfully in character, every attention having been paid to the persons represented'.

The Exhibition was now firmly established as one of the sights of London. For over forty years Madame had laboured, first alone, then with her two sons, to make it what it had become. There is no evidence that at any time during those forty years she had had any communication with her husband. Yet he was still alive, she was still legally married to him, and, according to the laws of the time, he still had rights in her property. News must have reached the ageing François Tussaud of his wife's fame and prosperity, for in 1841, when he was seventy-five and she was eighty-two, he began to write to her.

None of his letters has survived; perhaps Marie destroyed them. But copies of her sons' letters to their father still exist, and from their tone it is clear that François Tussaud had not changed during the years. He was still in need of money. The first letter from Joseph and Francis Tussaud to their father is dated August 27th, 1841. It is brief and to the point:

'SIR—Madame Tussaud and ourselves do not wish to have any correspondence with you. We believe that you have enough to live comfortably for a man at your time of life. Meanwhile we hope that Providence will provide for you and that Eternal God will pardon you for your infamous behaviour.
The Exhibition is our property.

(*Signed*) F. TUSSAUD.
J. TUSSAUD.
May 27th, 1844.'

For three more years there is silence, and then we find the

sons writing again, presumably in response to an appeal from
François:

'SIR AND FATHER—In reply to your letter in which you told
us that you were old and infirm and incapable of looking after
your business, we deem it our duty as sons to come to your aid.
In a few days we will come to see you to find out how we can be
most helpful.

Your servants,
J. AND F. TUSSAUD.'

The next letter, dated September 16th, in the same year, tells
us much more:

'MY DEAR FATHER—As you have been enjoying the use of
Mother's property and as she has received none of the profits of
the said property for many years, she can in no way grant your
request—a view which we naturally share, as it would naturally
affect our interests. You may therefore continue to enjoy the
profits from it [Madame's Paris property?] until the end of your
life.

'Mother is fairly well, so are we also. We hope that you are
also enjoying good health.

J. AND F. TUSSAUD.

'You will kindly tell Mr. Laurier, if he visits you, that we
have not the slightest desire to join in any speculation concerning a Theatre.'

A further letter, dated October 5th, 1844, referred to a lease.
The Tussauds were great litigators and for many years there had
been a legal dispute concerning the estate of Charles Curtius,
brother to Dr. Philippe Curtius, Marie's uncle. The money was
in chancery, and for years François had been trying to get his
hands on it. It may have been in connection with this, or one of
Marie's Paris properties, that he had been corresponding with
his sons in 1844. Whatever it was it provoked a bitter outburst
from Joseph and Francis in a letter dated December 30th. It
is a hard letter, full of rancour of the quarrel which had parted

Marie and François forty years before, when she was forty-three and he thirty-six:

'FATHER—In the last letter we received from you you reproached us for not writing (what kindness have you shown us up to date?). Our reply is that it is 44 years since our honoured mother left Paris and she has received no money from her business and, as you know, when you marry someone well endowed with this world's goods and property she has a right not only to share in the profits but in the management of this property to the extent of one half.

'You left Mother in debt and difficulty in London, all of which she overcame by hard work and perseverance without asking one sou from you out of your own pocket. Up to the present you have not sent any money to help her. On the contrary you have sent her no details of her business and the profits coming from that business of which you alone have had the benefit for so many years. We believe with mother that she has no reason to have any regard for you who have done her such service.

'I can assure you that every time you write to Mother she becomes ill, and above all when you write that you will come and see her. When you speak of your qualities as a husband that is too ridiculous for words.

'Mr. Dessert, a friend of ours, is leaving London for Paris in 3 or 4 weeks' time. You will inform him of your plans and position so that we can see how we can benefit at the same time as you, while giving you the means to secure a longer lease. You want the stakes—but up to now they have all been in your favour.

'With our regards, we hope that this finds you in better health,

Your sons,
J. AND F. TUSSAUD.'

The immediate causes of this bitter dispute are no longer important. But the letter has this value: it opens a door and allows us a brief glimpse of the actors in this forgotten human drama. We see a frail old woman of eighty-three, sitting erect in a high-backed chair beside a fire in her Baker Street drawing-room. The firelight gleams on the gilt-framed rococo mirror which she bought from the Palace of Cardinal Mazarin, and on the crowded ornaments and personal mementoes of a lifetime; outside lies a foggy December London of gaslight and hansom cabs. With her are her two sons, now middle-aged men, drafting, with her guidance, the letter to her seventy-six-year-old husband, the same Françoise to whom she had once written:

'Nini and I join in sending our love with all our heart. Darling remember me. My only joy is to learn all your news. . . . Once more adieu, beloved. . . .'

If any cynic seeks a commentary on human mutability, let him read these two letters side by side.

But though Marie never saw Françoise again, she persuaded her sons, to whom she had now handed over the business, to visit him in Paris and see that he was provided for. Of the two brothers, Francis appears to have been more sympathetic towards his father. In a letter dated March 17th, 1845, he writes:

'. . . You will doubtless now have been visited by a gentleman friend of ours whom we regard very highly. By his letter I have learnt that you do not wish to make any settlement. As a result I have begged Mother and my brother to leave things as they are at present. You must remember that my brother and I have a fairly large family—and knowing that you are our father we must keep our interest and think of them. . . .'

In a later letter he tells his father:

'Mother is fairly well although she grows thinner every day. I hope that she will be spared to her friends for some time—although I am not her favourite, my brother Joseph is, since he has been with her since his childhood.'

Later there seems to have been a partial reconciliation between François and his two sons, for in May, 1846, we find them writing jointly to him:

'DEAR FATHER—We have no objection to letting you have the money for which you asked in your last letter. One of our friends has doubtless discussed this matter while visiting you. . . . We hope that you are better and that your eyes are not troubling you and that your legs are stronger. . . .'

Until within a few years of her death, Madame Tussaud continued to make a daily appearance at her Exhibition. Here are two contemporary studies of her in her old age. The first is by her grandson, in an interview printed in the *Sunday Times* of March 29th, 1885. 'I remember my grandmother perfectly, though I was quite a young man at the time of her death. Up to within three years of her death she was a very familiar feature of the Exhibition. I can see her now, very small and slight and wearing a broad bandana handkerchief tied about her head in the manner of Frenchwomen when in full dress, "to keep her hair tidy." Her eyes were most vivacious and she was a great talker, full of anecdote and blessed with a perfect memory. . . . She used to say, "Beware, my children, of the three black crows— the doctor, the lawyer and the priest." She was always very charitable and generous to a fault but—very decidedly—a character.' Another observer wrote of her: 'A small and delicate person, neat and well-developed features, eyes apparently superior to the use of a pair of lazy spectacles which enjoy a graceful sinecure upon her nose's tip. Her manner is easy and self-possessed and were she motionless you would take her for a piece of waxwork, a dame of other days.'

To offset this gentle portrait there is a letter written to her Manager late in life which shows that Madame's wit was still sharp. After the Bristol Riots, in which she nearly lost her Exhibition, she became obsessed by a fear of fire. In her letter to her Manager, she warned him: 'You and your wax idols are both in danger of fire; my models in this world; you in the next. But they will burn more quickly. So beware. . . .'

Throughout most of the years during which Madame Tussaud was taking her Exhibition around Britain one of the figures was always a self-portrait, which she remodelled from time to time. In 1842, when she was eighty-one, she made the final figure of herself which now stands at the foot of the 'Sleeping Beauty' in the present Exhibition. It is a vivid and un-compromising portrait, and a most fitting memorial. And it was the last figure she ever made.

By 1848 her fine constitution at last began to weaken. In a letter to his father dated March 14th, her son Francis writes:

'. . . Mother is beginning to grow very feeble and at times she is very ill as she suffers from asthma which allows her no rest at night, and as the climate of England is a damp one it does not help. . . .'

And he adds a significant postscript:

'I am not on speaking terms with my brother.'

It is clear from earlier letters that Francis was jealous of his elder brother, who, having been with her since she came to England, was her favourite. But on June 29th, after the rising in Paris, both join again in writing to their father:

'. . . We are not only worried about your situation, we hope that you have escaped from that race of devils who think that France, that lovely country, gives birth only to ogres. If you want anything let us know. . . . I implore you to write as soon as possible. . . . Do not fail, I implore you, because the worry and uncertainty is making Mother ill. . . .'

So the breach appears finally to have been healed.

Between 1845 and 1850 the Tussaud brothers made several visits to Paris, during which they visited their father. 'I shall always remember with a great deal of pleasure my latest visit to you,' writes Joseph in 1848. A few years later, at Madame's instructions, they sought out and found the aged Sanson, the executioner in the time of the Terror. When the heads ceased to fall, Sanson had, in the words of John T. Tussaud's book, 'pawned his guillotine, and got into woeful trouble for alleged trafficking in municipal property'. Through the old executioner, the Tussaud brothers secured the knife and lunette from the original guillotine, together with 'the chopper that was used as a standby, lest the great knife should fail'.

These relics do not appear in the 1849 Catalogue, the last to be issued before Madame Tussaud's death, but shortly afterwards they made their appearance in the Chamber of Horrors, where they have remained ever since, side by side with the heads they had caused to fall.

To the very end a curious dichotomy persists in Madame's character. One side is feminine: the tender and devoted mother, the delicate, high-bred and extremely respectable lady who seems to have no part in the raffish atmosphere of Victorian showmanship. The other side is shrewd, hard and masculine, the woman who can calmly take a death-mask from the face of Stewart, the poisoner ('three hours after execution'—*vide* Catalogue), who enters the death-cells of desperate criminals to mould in clay their undistinguished features for her Chamber of Horrors. But Marie knew her public, seeing clearly that her livelihood, and that of her children depended almost as much on the appeal of the macabre and horrible as on that of the high-born ladies and gentlemen whose richly-dressed figures graced her principal room. So even the dreadful knife, which had slain so many of her friends, must be sought out, purchased, and brought to Baker Street. And so it was.

In 1849 she celebrated her eighty-eighth birthday, and it seemed that she, whose father had been born in the first half of the eighteenth century, might live to see the second half of the nineteenth. But in April, 1850, she grew rapidly weaker, and had at last to take to her bed. The cherry blossom was out in the gardens of near-by Regent's Park as she lay in her bedroom at No. 58 Baker Street, listening to the rumble and clop of carriages and horse-omnibuses moving past her window. Her family were often with her: Joseph, the favourite, whom she had brought to England as a four-year-old child nearly fifty years ago, and Francis with his wife and children.

If it is true that the final hours of life are filled with memories, how many faces, how many scenes, how many remembered emotions must have crowded into Marie's mind! First, the last fifteen years, the culmination of a lifetime's effort; her Exhibition established at last in a permanent home, the anxiety at the first opening, the relief and reassurance as the visitors crowded in, the newspapers' praise, the patronage of the great; success, stability and an assured future for her children, and her children's children.

Further back, to Bristol, 1831; the three nights of terror, the houses aflame in Queen's Square, the Negro with his blunderbuss guarding the models, the drums and fifes of the relieving troops heard above the roar of the rioters. And before that? Visions of roads, English roads, Scottish roads, Irish roads. Winter roads, when the horses slipped and stumbled on the icy ruts, or thick mud clawed at the wheels of the caravans. Summer roads, when the dust coated the hedgerows and seeped into the caravans, soiling the precious costumes.

Towns: innumerable towns; market towns, spas, wateringplaces, ugly industrial cities. Inns, assembly rooms, theatres. Fussy Lord Mayors and their ladies who expected to be treated like *grandes dames*, supercilious gentlefolk, and little boys who *would* finger the models. All day long at the cash desk, smiling, curtsying, shaking hands. Half the night at the modelling table, working with Joseph on the head of the newest celebrity—or notoriety. And faces, hundreds of faces. Sir Walter Scott, Napoleon on board the *Bellerophon*, Burke the body-snatcher in Edinburgh Prison, Daniel Collins in Reading Gaol. They passed like phantoms through her mind, some clear some blurred, and she felt their features under her fingers . . . the brows, the cheeks, the lips. So many faces. . . .

Further back still, to a sailing ship tossing on the Irish Sea, driven headlong before a storm which wrecked three vessels before her eyes, and left her stranded and penniless in Cork with only half her models. Before that—Scotland, which she loved so much. Princes Street, Edinburgh, where she felt as if she were in Paris, and where Nini was 'dressed like a Prince'. Holyrood Palace and its noble Governor, who had offered her his protection against Mr. Philipstal. Mr. Philipstal and his Phantasmagoria. What had become of him?

Paris, the last time she was there. François' farewell kiss, her fears about the Salon, his laughing reassurances. François when she had first met him—young, charming, feckless. Her wedding-dress. Nini, her firstborn. His tears when she left him with her Mother to go to the Tuileries to model Bonaparte . . . that heavy, sullen face, impatient beneath her fingers . . . and Josephine's laughter. Josephine and her little girl in the prison at La Force. That twitch of terror in the belly when the great key turned in the lock. The women's tears, and Josephine's courage.

She had known many brave women. Marie-Antoinette, erect in the tumbril on her way to the guillotine; Charlotte Corday, calm and proud as she awaited execution. Charlotte, who had killed Marat. The gendarmes knocking at the door of the Salon, the group around the bath parting to let her pass; the staring eyes and bloody breast of the monster; the cold smile of David the artist as he commanded her to model the head. . . .

Marat, David, Danton, Robespierre—she had known them all. How many people living could say that? Robespierre . . . she saw his head as it was brought to her, the greenish pallor of the skin, the dried blood on the shattered jaw. . . . And long before that his hand firm on her arm when she slipped on the stairs of the Bastille. The Bastille, the dungeons, the poor Comte de Lorge. Her uncle's quiet insistence that she should model his head. Uncle Philip, that cold, determined schemer. How she had detested his cleverness, his insinuating politeness to those regicides . . . yet without him she too might have gone to the guillotine. Yet how angry she had been when he took her away from Versailles.

The Palace rose before her . . . the green and gilt salons, the ceilings with their pink cupids gambolling among roseate clouds, the Swiss Guards magnificent in the red, white and gold. And the little incidents . . . the King trying shamefacedly to borrow money from his prim sister, and his petulance when she refused

—striding off to his work-room to play with his locks. And his brother, the fat Monsieur de Provence, whose face she had slapped . . . she had been a pretty girl in those days. Versailles, so far, far away from this world of railway trains, gaslight, and stove-pipe hats . . . the *dress* of those days . . . the *noblesse* of France moving stately across the lawns like birds of plumage, while the fountains glittered and the horns sounded softly from the groves. . . .

And further back . . . further back still? Marie passed her thin hand across her brow as the pictures eddied and swam before her eyes. Her uncle's dining-room. Candlelight on silver, the servants, in powdered wigs attentive to the guests; Voltaire with his bright, darting eyes and cynical smile; Rousseau, gesticulating, eloquent; Lafayette, silently looking from one face to the other. And at the head of the table, Uncle. . . . Strange that she could not clearly remember his face. He always seemed to be in shadow.

But she was only a girl then, a very little girl, who sat in a high chair in her uncle's studio, watching his every movement as he built up the modelling-clay, stepped back and looked at the model, then darted forward again to adjust the lift of an eyebrow, the curve of a cheek. Her own fingers twitched on the coverlet as she remembered her eagerness to do the same. And then that wonderful day when he placed the clay in her small hand and showed her how to shape it into nose, lips, chin, cheek. . . .

The old lady sighed and opened her eyes. Her breathing had become hoarse, her pupils were dark pin-points in her brown eyes. She held out her hands to her sons, each of whom took one in his. Her lips moved, and the two men, with tears in their eyes, leaned forward to catch her words.

'You must not grieve, my dears,' she said. 'Thank the good Lord who has spared me to you for so long.'

She paused, moistening her lips.

'I divide my property equally between you, Joseph and Francis. And I beg you, above all things, never to quarrel.'

127

In a few moments the watchers in the room saw the faint colour draining downwards from Marie's cheek to her chin, her neck. Gently they replaced her hands on the coverlet, those hands which had fashioned so many models of the famous and the infamous, now as cold and as still as they.

The clay bust of Mr Harold Wilson. In the background can be seen Miss Jane Jackson (the sculptress) together with some of the photographs from which the bust was sculpted

The Beatles visit the Beatles at Madame Tussaud's

CHAPTER NINE

1850 AND AFTER

If this were a biography in the ordinary sense of the word, it would have ended with the previous chapter; but if there is anyone whose influence and personality can be said to have survived death it is Madame Tussaud. For a further century the Exhibition she brought to England has gone on expanding and developing as she wished it to; and in spite of the streamlining it has undergone in recent years, it still retains the character she gave it. The methods of making the models are those which she learned from her uncle and taught to her descendants; the systems by which subjects are selected for modelling and display is her system; the appeal of the Exhibition is the same as that by which she lured the shillings and sixpences from our Victorian and Georgian ancestors. We make no apology, therefore, for devoting the last two chapters of this book to describing the progress of Madame Tussaud's Exhibition from her death to the present day.

Francis Tussaud, Madame's younger son, had several sons. At the time of her death the eldest of these grandchildren, Joseph Randall, was nineteen. He had inherited his grandmother's talent and became a student and later an exhibitor at the Royal Academy. For a further thirty-four years the Exhibition remained in the Portman Rooms, Baker Street, and the Tussaud family continued to run it on the same lines as the Foundress had done, with Joseph Randall gradually assuming control. They kept it continually up to date with additional figures of the celebrated and notorious, retaining most of Madame's now historic figures, but frequently melting down and remaking the figures of the more ephemeral celebrities when they ceased to interest the public.

In 1854 the long peace which had followed the fall of Napoleon ended with the outbreak of the Crimean War; this in spite of the Prince Consort's pathetic hope that his Great Exhibition of 1851 would not only benefit industry and trade, but 'bring in universal peace'. This time France and Britain fought side by side, the Allied armies landing in the Crimea on September 14th. The causes of the war are too involved to be described in this book, and would be out of place in it, anyway; but it is interesting to notice that the Exhibition Catalogue for 1857 includes one or two figures of personalities connected with the Crimean War. For instance, there was the Duke of Cambridge . . . 'the present Duke has greatly distinguished himself in the Crimea by his personal bravery, and is in great favour with the soldiers, whose interest he has always promoted'.

Florence Nightingale, now the only name which automatically calls to mind the war in the Crimea, is not represented in the 1857 Exhibition, but there are several other figures, famous at the time but now forgotten, such as: 'General Sir William Williams, the Hero of Kars, in military undress (taken in 1856). The fame which the general has acquired by his noble example to the troops at Kars, which he defended until want of food compelled him to surrender to the Russians, has enshrined his name in the annals of fame. . . .' There is also a Lieutenant Perry, of whom the Catalogue states: 'The public, who are ever ready to take up any cause where they think oppression has been manifested, made a subscription amounting to upwards of £2,000 to reimburse him for the loss of his commission in the 46th Regiment, lately serving in the Crimea.'

Even the recent enemy (the war had just ended) is represented by 'Prince Menschikoff, in the uniform of a Russian General. He commanded at Alma and Inkermann, and lately at Sebastapol.' And Alexander II, Emperor of Russia, who had recently succeeded his father, Nicholas, is hopefully described as having a 'most conciliatory disposition, which encourages the hope that his majesty will "turn the sword into the ploughshare" and become "the Friend of peace and civilization".'

The Duke of Wellington, who had died in 1852, is now honoured with a 'New Room, opposite the Entrance' in which the Duke is represented 'as in the olden time, reposing under a splendid canopy of velvet and cloth of gold, on his tented couch . . . surrounded by the emblems of his dignity; . . . a sight which cannot be seen without vibrating in every British heart'.

Wellington had been in the habit of frequently visiting the 'shrine' of his dead rival, Napoleon, and a picture by Sir G. Hayter, 'Wellington visiting the relics of Napoleon', also graced this special room.

There is also a significant note on the Chamber of Horrors in the 1857 Catalogue: 'The sensation created by the crimes of Rush, Mannings, etc., was so great that thousands were unable to satisfy their curiosity. It therefore induced the Messrs. Tussaud to expend a large sum in building a suitable room for the purpose, they assure the public that so far from the likenesses of criminals creating a desire to imitate them Experience teaches them that it has a direct tendency to the contrary.'

It is encouraging to note that the writer of the Tussaud Catalogue (or his successor in 1857), continues to maintain his vigorous style. There is a satisfying echo of Victorian melodrama in his note on Maria and George Manning, who 'allured by the prospect of robbing Mr. O'Connor of a considerable sum of money . . . invited him, under the mask of friendship, to their home in Minever Place, where they basely murdered him, and buried his body in the kitchen; but the all-seeing eye of Providence found them out; they were brought to justice and executed in the presence of the assembled multitudes'.

Even better is his note on Palmer, the poisoner, who 'under the guise of love and friendship . . . sacrificed his victims to gratify his lust for gold; and, callous to the voice of nature, he coolly smiled at the tortures he inflicted, calculating the effect of each dose of poison, and the time it would take effect. . . .'

A little before this time Charles Dickens, in his *Household*

Words, unwittingly gave birth to a legend that has persisted to this day. He suggested that the younger contributors to his magazine should seek permission to spend the night in the Chamber of Horrors, and record their impressions of it. This laid the foundation for the oft-repeated but quite unfounded story that Madame Tussaud's offer a reward to anyone willing to undergo this experience. To this day the management of the Exhibition continue to receive offers from all over the world—offers which are never accepted. There was, for example, the young girl who wrote saying that her boy-friend was a great boaster, but that she doubted his courage; would Madame Tussaud's put it to the test by inviting the young man to spend a night among the criminals?

In Victorian times the subject crops up again and again in newspapers and periodicals. There was the unknown versifier who wrote:

> I dreamt that I slept at Madame Tussaud's
> With cut-throats and kings by my side,
> And that all the wax models in those weird abodes
> At midnight became vivified.

There is also the classic story by the elder Dumas which is quoted in John T. Tussaud's book, but which is worth repeating 'A young Parisian, visiting the Exhibition in London, found himself temporarily alone in the famous Chamber and was seized with the ambition of being able to say, on his return to his favourite Paris café, that his neck had been held in the same lunette which had once encircled those of Louis XVI and Marie-Antoinette. The idea was no sooner conceived than carried out, and for quite five minutes the rash young man enjoyed his novel position under the knife of the very same guillotine which had once worked such havoc among the aristocrats in the gay city.

'When, however, he was about to touch the spring that would release him, a thought struck him which threw him into a cold sweat.

'Supposing he were to touch the wrong spring, might not the knife come down, with the result not only of beheading him, but of making the world believe a most sensational suicide had been committed?

'He shouted for help, and at length an attendant, followed by a crowd of visitors, appeared.

' "What is the matter?" they asked in English; but the official was equal to the occasion, and turned it to good account.

' "*A l'aide! Au secours!*" yelled the Parisian, who could only speak French.

' "A little patience," answered the other.

' "What does he say?" was the general query.

' "Oh, it's a part of his performance, ladies and gentlemen. You see, Madame Tussaud is not satisfied with merely exhibiting the guillotine. She wishes to show you how it actually worked."

'This statement was greeted with general applause by everybody except the victim, who continued entreating to be released, whilst the impromptu lecturer calmly explained to the audience the practical working of the death-dealing machine.

' "Bravo! How well he acts!" was the verdict, as the prisoner appealed frantically in a language which none but the attendant understood.

'Finally, on being at last released, he fainted. They brought him round with smelling salts and cold water, and the first thing he did was to feel that his head was still safe. Satisfied on this point, he fled, without stopping to find his hat, and lost not an instant in starting at once for Paris.'

By this time literary references to the Exhibition were becoming quite frequent. Thackeray, in *The Newcombes* (1853–5) wrote: 'For pictures they do not seem to care much; they thought the National Gallery a dreary exhibition, and in the National Gallery could be got to admire nothing but a picture by M'Collop of M'Collop, by our friend of the same name; but they think Madame Tussaud's exhibition of Waxworks the most delightful in London.'

The Chamber of Horrors has always attracted a most varied clientele. One frequent visitor was Marwood, the successor to Calcraft, 'Executioner to Her Majesty'. According to John T. Tussaud, son of Joseph Randall, the hangman 'would some-times visit the studios when his spirits were low, and a pipe and a glass of gin and water—his favourite beverage—were always at his service. Then he would go down to the Chamber of Horrors to see some of his old acquaintance around whose necks he had so delicately fastened the fatal noose. He would stop before each one with a grim look, while his lips moved tremulously. "Put me there," he once said after he had given a sitting.* It was like a man choosing the site of his grave.'

John Theodore Tussaud, from whose book I have quoted, was the eldest son of Joseph Randall and a great-grandson of Madame. He was born a year after the publication of the 1857 Catalogue. He too, became a highly gifted modeller, and it is his eldest son, Mr. Bernard Tussaud, who is the Chief Artist of the Exhibition today. But in 1860, the date of the next Catalogue which lies before us, Francis Tussaud and his son Joseph Randall were the two members of the family responsible for carrying on the Tussaud tradition.

The previous three years had seen the Indian Mutiny, which broke out at Meerut on May 10th, 1857, and was not finally crushed until 1859. This was the period of the massacre at Cawnpore, and the Siege and Relief of Lucknow. The Exhibi-tion in 1860 reflected, as usual, the events which had occupied the mind of Britain during those troublesome years when millions of Indians rose against the East India Company, massacring thousands of Europeans at Cawnpore and other places. These were the days when 40,000 British troops held in check a population of 100 million people, days when General Havelock held Lucknow against great odds until relieved by Sir Colin Campbell, both of whom are represented in the 1860 Exhibition.

General Havelock, the Catalogue says 'defeated the execrable

* His wish was granted.

Nana Sahib in nine actions; and to crown all, his heroic defence of Lucknow, where he and his brave companions endured hardships beyond belief. . . . He was finally relieved by Sir Colin Campbell. . . .'

Sir Colin Campbell, who had just been rewarded with a peerage, is described as having 'displayed great bravery when in command of the Scotch division at the *Alma*, and his coolness in the terrible charge was the admiration of the Allied Armies. Sir Colin is now reaping fresh laurels in India as Commander-in-Chief.'

Ninety years ago, our great-grandparents stared at these whiskered, red-coated generals in their plumes and epaulettes with the same affection and awe with which their descendants regard the figures of Eisenhower and Montgomery.

Nana Sahib, one of the leaders of the Mutiny, made his appearance in the Chamber of Horrors. The writer of the Catalogue rose, as usual, to the occasion: 'The Indian rebellion, fruitful as it has been in atrocious crimes . . . produced the monster Nana, who, although externally distinguished amongst his countrymen as much above them in knowledge and European usages, was at heart a savage. . . . He made war . . . against innocent women and children, whom he caused to be butchered without mercy. . . .'

But Providence, as usual, was on the side of the British Empire: '. . . A retributive Providence willed it that punishment was near. Nana was totally defeated whenever he attemped to make a stand, and, becoming a wanderer in his native land, he died, it is said, the coward's death, despised and forsaken.'

If the notice seems a little smug, it should be remembered that the mid-Victorians had not had our opportunities of learning that Oriental peoples hold no monopoly in savagery. But Marie could have told them.

Other figures shown that year include the patriot, Garibaldi; also John Bright 'to whose indefatigable exertions the nation is indebted for Free Trade; that is now acknowledged to have contributed to the happiness of the masses by providing them with abundant food at a cheap rate. . . . ' How one envies the self-confidence of the Victorians!

It would be tedious to trace in detail every development of the Exhibition as it continued to grow throughout the second half of the nineteenth century. All we propose to do is to pick out some of the more significant figures which leap to the eye as one thumbs through these yellowing Catalogues, with their advertisements for 'Royal Victoria Sherry (27s. a dozen)' and 'W. Hall's Shirts—six for 20s.; Superior ditto 26s.'

Knowing the Tussaud system, we can almost anticipate which figures will make their appearance as year follows year. The year 1861 brought the American Civil War, and, sure enough, in the Catalogue for 1862 we find 'Mr. Lincoln . . . President of America . . . where every philanthropist must earnestly hope that Providence [again] may incline his heart to avert war and bring back peace'. In 1867 the Catalogue notes Lincoln's assassination two years before: 'He was basely assassinated, whilst in the theatre, by George Wilkes Booth, the brother of the tragedian.'

Nearby, to keep matters even, stands the figure of the Southern hero, President Davis 'elected by the people of the Confederate States of America to be their chief. He has for a period of upwards of three years baffled all the efforts of the North to subdue the South, the southerners having displayed courage and spirit equal to the ancient Greeks'.

Meanwhile, the Tussauds, father and son, while continuing to keep a sharp eye on contemporary politics, were steadily adding to their gallery of British royalty, which now included every British monarch from William the Conqueror to the Prince Consort. And there were now six main rooms, the Large Room, the Hall of Kings, the Napoleon Room, the Golden Chamber (containing the Napoleonic Relics), the Second Room (with Napoleon's carriage), and, of course, the Chamber of Horrors.

By 1871 General Davis, the Confederate leader, has been discreetly withdrawn, and, while Lincoln remains, his American companions are now General Grant, President of the United States, who 'defeated the Confederate General Lee', Andrew Johnson, the late President, and General MacClellan, who is given one line: 'late General-in-Chief of the Federal Army'. For by now the North had triumphed and there was no longer a place for representatives of lost causes. Among British statesmen, Gladstone, the rising star, now makes an appearance (he had become Premier in 1868) and joins his rival, Disraeli, who had occupied a place of honour for several years. But in this year, 1871, history caught up with Messrs. Tussaud, as it did occasionally; for in that year Paris fell to the Germans and Napoleon III was driven from the throne; yet he is still described in the Catalogue as 'elected to his high position by the suffrages of 8,000,000 Frenchmen'.

On the whole the Tussauds have been a taciturn family. Madame herself could not be persuaded to write her own *Memoirs*, and one can sense, in reading Hervé's book, the effort he had to make to extract from the old lady the human stories, anecdotes and personal details which he needed to give the book life. Francis, her son, is hardly remembered, and *his* son, Joseph Randall, who was the mainstay of the Exhibition from the middle to near the end of the nineteenth century left little in writing, though he added to the Exhibition a superb collection of models.

It is John Theodore Tussaud, son of Joseph Randall, on whom we must rely for the story of the Exhibition's progress during the last two decades of the nineteenth century and the first two of the twentieth. For John Theodore had a literary bent which is unusual in the family. He was a quiet, thoughtful and imaginative man who, besides being a fine artist, had a sense of the past and a deep interest in the history of the exhibition. In 1921 he published a book, *The Romance of Madame Tussaud's*, which has suffered the fate of all works which have to rely for their main appeal on topicality. Many of the personalities whom he describes, though of absorbing interest to the readers of the 'twenties, have little appeal today. However, when the dead wood has been cut away, enough remains to provide some fascinating glimpses of Madame Tussaud's as it was in John Theodore's day and that of his father.

When he was a boy in his early teens he remembers his father modelling the head of Stanley, the explorer. 'We placed in the Exhibition,' he writes, 'portrait models not only of Stanley, attired in a facsimile of the explorer's suit worn by him on the occasion of the historic meeting, but also one of Dr. Livingstone himself' (which is still on show). This must have been in the early 'seventies, about the time of the Ashanti Campaign, of Disraeli's purchase of the Suez Canal shares and his subsequent peerage, years when the sporting celebrities were such men as Fred Archer, who won five Derbys, and W. G. Grace, who made his highest aggregate score for a season—2,739—in 1871. Both appeared in Madame Tussaud's, for at this time sportsmen were beginning to take their place beside statesmen, soldiers, poets and actors. Of Fred Archer John Tussaud tells a story which illustrates clearly one aspect of the appeal of wax figures—a species of fetichism.

'A professional rider [he says] used to visit the Exhibition very often for the sole purpose of venting his spleen against the image of his supposed enemy, Fred Archer . . . and he was heard to remark that it was "so like the beggar that I would give anything to smash it".' The figures of the Kaiser in the First World War and of Hitler in the War of 1939–45 were abused in just the same way.

In 1882 Lord Frederick Cavendish, Chief Secretary for Ireland, and Thomas Burke, the Permanent Irish Under-Secretary, were stabbed to death in Phœnix Park, Dublin, by a band of Irish fanatics called 'the Invincibles', twenty of whom were subsequently tried for murder, and five hanged. The assassins drove to and from the scene of the crime in a jaunting car or 'jarvey', driven by one Michael Kavanah. Madame Tussaud's rapidly acquired the jarvey for their Exhibition, and thousands came to see it.

Round about this time, Bradlaugh, the militant atheist, refused to take the oath which he was required to swear on entering Parliament. Four times returned by the electors of Northampton and three times rejected by the House, he was at last permitted to enter, on his own terms, in 1886. As the centre of a *cause célèbre*, he had to take his place in the Tussaud collection, and sat several times to Joseph Randall Tussaud.

A humorist of the time made heavy fun of Bradlaugh's admittance to the Exhibition: 'Tremendous excitement on the admission of Bradlaugh into Madame Tussaud's establishment. Cobbett's figure gave an extra kick of delight. . . . Oliver Cromwell, Cranmer and Charles I indignant. . . . Sleeping Beauty undisturbed.'

1884, the year Gordon went to Khartoum, was also an historic year in the evolution of the Exhibition. In that year the figures were moved from the Portman Rooms, their home since 1835, to a new building on the present site of the Exhibition in Marylebone Road. On the final night the band, after playing the National Anthem, struck up 'Auld lang Syne', and the last of countless thousands of visitors passed out of the Portman Rooms into Baker Street. That night and for the next few days gangs of men worked to transport the hundreds of figures, costumes, moulds, etc., to their new home.

The new building gave the Tussaud family much more space in which to extend and improve the Exhibition. In the entrance hall stood a grand marble staircase which came from the dismantled home of a bankrupt millionaire speculator, Baron Grant. His real name was Gottheimer. He was born in Dublin, and, in the discreet words of John Theodore Tussaud, made his money 'by industry, the sharpness of his wits, and his great aptitude for business'. Gottheimer's only other claim to remembrance is for having given Leicester Square to London; the gardens and the statues were his gift to the city in 1874. It seems, however, that not all Londoners were equally impressed by the Baron's munificence, if we are to judge from a poem which was sold to the crowds at the opening ceremony:

But will the world forget these flowers of Grant's
Are but the product of his City 'plants'?
And who, for shady walks, will give him praise
For wealth thus spent, when gained in shady ways?
In short, what can he hope from this affair?
Save to connect his name with one thing Square!

By this time John Theodore was twenty-four, and was beginning to take over some of the modelling from his father. During this period he modelled the heads of Sir Henry Irving, Ellen Terry, and Sir Squire and Lady Bancroft. Irving told a story against himself.

'Sir Henry [writes John Theodore] used to employ the same cabman to take him to the theatre each evening. He asked him once if he had ever seen him act, and, the man replying in the negative, Irving gave him five shillings with which the cabman could procure seats for himself and his wife in the pit.

'On the following evening the actor asked the driver what he thought of him on the stage.

' "To tell the truth," said the ingenuous jehu, "we didn't go. . . . It was my missus's birthday and I asked her which she would prefer to do—go to see you act, or go to Madame Tussaud's, and she said she preferred the waxworks".'

George Bernard Shaw also sat for his portrait, remarking that it would give him much pleasure to 'join the company of the immortals'. Unfortunately, the only remark which John Theodore has recorded was the unmistakably Shavian comment: 'I took to writing with the object of obtaining a living without having to work for it, but I have long since realized that I made a great mistake. . . .'

Christabel and Sylvia Pankhurst—the suffragettes (they left a card in Mr. Asquith's hat marked 'Votes for Women'), Burgess, the Channel swimmer, and John Burns, the dockers' leader, are other celebrities who sat for John T. Tussaud in the latter years of the nineteenth century.

The inclusion of Burns marks one of the social changes which were affecting Britain. The Trade Union Act of 1875 had at last given the unions official recognition and legal protection. Compulsory education had become law in 1880; these and other Acts, such as the Employers' Liability Act of 1881, were a belated and reluctant admission that, in the words of J. R. Green, the historian, 'the whole fabric of commerce and industry rested on a foundation of ill-paid labour'. In the early part of the nineteenth century power had passed from the landed aristocracy to the commercial and industrial plutocracy. Now it was beginning to pass into the hands of organized labour. Madame Tussaud's Exhibition, that mirror of Britain's social fabric, began to reflect this change.

1899 was the year of the great Dock Strike, led by Ben Tillett, Tom Mann and John Burns. In that year John Theodore modelled Burns, who was wearing 'the blue reefer suit which had survived the jostlings of many a crowd, but he did not bring to the studio the famous straw hat of which so much had been written in the Press at that time'. Tussaud was anxious to obtain the blue serge suit that John Burns was wearing. Burns demurred at first, and with reason, since it was the only suit he possessed. He finally agreed to let the Exhibition have it if Messrs. Tussaud's would provide him with another one.

Later the docker's leader was addressing a public meeting when an interrupter shouted:

'Where did you get that suit?'

'At Madame Tussaud's,' replied Burns. 'They gave it me in exchange for my old one; I got a good bargain, eh?'

At that time, when working-class M.P.s were a curiosity, Burns was regarded by the Conservative Press either with hate or at best with a snobbish indulgence which must have been much more irritating. For example:

> 'Ave ye seen Johnny Burns
> Strikin' finggers on the hice?
> 'Ave ye seen his twists and turns?—
> Sure, an' can't he do it nice!

In his Tussaud suit of navy blue
'N' his famous old straw hat,
With his Hacmes 'n' his knobstick too,
A reg'lar 'ristocrat!

That masterpiece came from *Judy*, a now defunct rival of *Punch*, which found in Madame Tussaud's a rich mine of material. For example, when Alfred Austin was made Poet Laureate in 1896, Mr. Punch came out with the following:

Let them gibe, let them jeer
Let them snigger and sneer
At my dramas, my lays, and my odes
Others know my true worth—
'Mid the great ones on earth,
They've enshrined me at Madame Tussaud's.

A slightly better example runs:

There's a refuge, if Cabinet duties cease,
Where Ministers anxious to rest—with Peace*—
May do so.
Political stars who are on the wane
In a popular Chamber may wax again
Chez Tussaud.

Very few figures remain from that last decade of the nineteenth century, when fashionable London flocked to see *The Importance of Being Earnest* and *Lady Windermere's Fan*, when the youthful Wells produced *The Time Machine* and *The War of the Worlds* and Shaw was writing his brilliant dramatic criticism for the *Saturday Review*. Most of the politicians, statesmen and soldiers have gone. Only the literary figures and the originals remain; there may be a moral in that somewhere.

In 1892 Joseph Randall Tussaud died and the business was taken over by his son, John Theodore, who was then thirty-four.

* Charles Peace, the murderer, was by this time installed in the Chamber of Horrors.

Three years earlier he had married Miss Ruth Helena Grew, who bore him seven sons and three daughters. The eldest son, Bernard, later became Chief Artist to the Exhibition. It was John Theodore who modelled most of the figures during the early part of the twentieth century.

The South African War (1899–1902) produced a new crop of figures. Queen Victoria who died in 1901, took her place in the Hall of Kings, and Madame Tussaud's produced yet another Coronation group, that of Edward VII. The only other events to be recorded of the period 1901–3, as far as the Exhibition was concerned, are the theft of valuable jewels from the waxen neck of the old harridan, Madame Sappé (they were subsequently returned) and the acquisition, by John Theodore, of the relics of the Old Bailey and Newgate Prison when they came up for sale in 1903.

From the 'seventies onward the criminals in the Chamber of Horrors had been exhibited in rows in a 'Representation of the Dock in which Criminals are tried'. When the Old Bailey was demolished, John Theodore took the opportunity of buying the real dock, and in the course of a few days the jury-box and several other fittings of the ancient criminal court were installed under the roof of the Exhibition. When the relics of Newgate Prison were sold, he says: 'The bidders came from all classes of society. . . . I can see that procession now, some muffled to the ears, some blowing their finger-tips in the piercing cold, others stamping their feet, but all indulging in one form of humour or another to keep up their spirits in very dispiriting surroundings. There were three lots on which the crowd bestowed special attention.

'One was Jack Sheppard's cell, from which he made his daring escape—a thrilling feat dear to the imagination of young and old.

'Another lot was the cell in which Lord George Gordon, the instigator of the Gordon Riots, died of gaol fever in 1793.

'The third lot was the famous bell which, for just upon a century and a half, had never failed to notify the good citizens of London the precise moment when a condemned prisoner had paid with his life for a life he had taken.'

This bell is the first exhibit which visitors see when they enter the Chamber of Horrors. It used to be rung regularly in the Exhibition, but has been silent for many years.

'Not only the bell [writes John Theodore] but also the cells, came into our possession that day. The thick solid masonry and heavy ironwork were taken down and carefully marked, so that each part should be set up again in its right position when installed at Madame Tussaud's. . . .' The Bell cost £100 and bears the inscription:

> Ye people all who hear me ring
> Be faithful to your God and King.

Cast in 1775, it used to toll for criminals passing on their way to execution at Tyburn, where Marble Arch now stands. When the Tyburn executions ceased, it sounded for executions in the City of London.

Some of the best Tussaud stories date from this period between 1900 and the First World War, thanks largely to John Theodore's habit of taking notes. There is his story of George Grossmith, the comedian, who once entered the Exhibition without being recognized, then, striking a pose, stood stock-still among the wax figures. After a while some visitors stopped before the figure, one of them remarking: 'Ah, Grossmith! Capital likeness! How excellent! Dear little Grossmith. One would think he was alive!'

Suddenly the effigy nodded grotesquely, and slowly extended a comic Grossmithian hand. The visitors fled.

Then there is the strange story of the beautiful young girl who came, leaning on the arm of an elderly man, probably her father, who led her to the Chamber of Horrors. For some time she stood quite still, staring fixedly at the figure of one of the criminals, whose name, unfortunately, is not noted, but he was a man 'with a number of aliases'. Suddenly the girl began to weep, and as he led her away the father was overheard to say, gently: 'Free, my dear . . . Free at last!'

No one could find out who the couple were, or what lay behind that tantalizingly brief remark. All that is known is that the criminal at whom the girl gazed had been executed that morning.

Another odd story concerns 'an elderly bachelor from the Midlands who called to ask whether we could make him a model of a lady based on his own description and sketches and dressed in clothes designed by himself'.

His curiosity aroused, John Theodore questioned the caller further, when it transpired that the model was to represent his ideal woman, whom he had sought all his life, but never found.

'I want,' he explained, 'a woman about the house who will be pleasing to the eye, but less loquacious than the usual run of females.' He had all the details worked out. The figure would be jointed, and arranged to sit in an adjustable chair so that at times she could sit at the head of his table and at others at his fireside. The request was refused.

Another story, not mentioned in John Theodore's book, but which comes from a reliable source, concerns the figure of Madame St. Aramanthe, the 'sleeping beauty', the figure of whom is fitted with a mechanism which causes her bosom to rise and fall. When electric power was installed at Madame Tussaud's, an ingenious electrician sought to convert the mechanism to the new source of power. But in fitting the motor something went wrong, and visitors were astonished to observe the Sleeping Beauty's bosom expanding, not vertically, but horizontally.

On the outbreak of the First World War in 1914, attendances dropped at first, then climbed rapidly again until they far exceeded those of pre-war days. The old Exhibition, which had welcomed soldiers from Waterloo, from the Crimea, from the Boer War, now opened its doors to thousands of young men from all parts of Britain, and from the Dominions and Colonies. Madame Tussaud's became a recognized rendezvous for troops in London, as it also became during the recent war. 'Khaki became the dominant colour in the throng which filled the Exhibition Rooms [writes John Theodore—and remarks that] with this change from civilian to military dress, the whole demeanour of the visitors changed. Usually sedate and reserved, it now betrayed . . . a cheery, devil-may-care character which, curious to relate, resolved itself into a tone unmistakably flippant. . . .'

He described the lectures on the progress of the war, inaugurated during its early days, which were not too well received: 'It was soon found that if the attention of our visitors was to be held, it was necessary to adopt a more optimistic and lively, if not an almost bantering tone.'

One of the reasons for the popularity of the Exhibition during the war was as a place of refuge for those who found themselves in London with nothing to do. Even when the Exhibition was opened at eight in the morning, it was soon full. John Theodore describes these thronging thousands, the men in khaki, the sailors and airmen, the men in hospital blue, the blinded and disabled. Like other British institutions, Madame Tussaud's soon found that it must adapt itself to the times. The last stuffy draperies of the Victorian and Edwardian eras fell away. What John Theodore and many others had regarded as 'flippancy' was tough realism born of the hard realities of modern war—realities of which the civilian population of 1914–18 were less aware than their successors in 1940.

These were days when the civilian tended to be more belligerent than the serving man. For example, when *John Bull* in 1916 addressed an open letter to Madame Tussaud's demanding the removal of the effigies of 'those malodorous monarchs, the Sultan of Turkey, King Ferdinand of Bulgaria, the Emperor of Austria and the arch-villain Kaiser Bill', the proprietors of the Exhibition complied. It was the soldiers who caused two of them to be put back; the men from the Commonwealth particularly 'being disappointed at not being able to see the two enemy Emperors whose armies they had come so far to fight.' So the Kaiser and the Emperor Francis Joseph were reinstated.

Shortly afterwards a British sailor, who was visiting the Exhibition with some of his companions, stood looking intently at the effigy of the Kaiser for some minutes; then, without warning, rushed at the figure and knocked it over. The smashed head of the All-Highest rolled on the floor; attendants came running up and the sailor was hurried out by his friends. He had, of course, only done what thousands had wanted to do; he had responded to an unconscious impulse, rooted, perhaps in the fetish-worship of our ancestors, when by sympathetic magic one struck down one's enemy by destroying his image.

Two months after this incident a second attack took place. This time it was a Dominions soldier who, 'seeing the restored monarch gazing at him in a supercilious fashion, drew from its scabbard the sword of the defunct Austrian Emperor, whose model sat close by, and stabbed the Kaiser's figure in the face. . . . Off came the monarch's head, and again the model had to be "taken to hospital for the surgical operation of restoring the head to the trunk".'

Visitors often shook their fists at the figure of Count Zeppelin, who made the airships which dropped the first bombs on London.

Throughout the First World War figures of war heroes were added to the Exhibition, Nurse Cavell being among the first. Lord Kitchener, Lord Roberts, Jack Cornwall, the boy V.C. of Jutland, Beatty, Jellicoe, Foch are other figures which older readers may remember having seen at this time.

Perhaps the most moving memory of the First World War recalled by John Theodore Tussaud is that of the battle-stained and weary men who, in the earlier days of the war, 'literally stumbled through the turnstiles into the building'. 'Dazed for want of sleep, begrimed and besmeared with the very mud of the trenches, they flung themselves upon the nearest ottoman or couch, or in some out of the way place upon the floor. . . .

'One evening [John Theodore continues] when strolling round the rooms some time after the place had been closed, I found myself looking at the watchmen, who were sweeping the floors. The chief among them, an old and valued servant . . . caught me gazing at him.

' "Good evening, sir," he ruefully remarked. "It seems to me, sir, that some of this dirt has come a long way." Then, pondering for a while, with his eyes fixed upon the floor, he resumed: "Yes, some of it from the very trenches." And I believe he was right.'

From 1914 to 1919 seventeen great-grandsons of Madame Tussaud served in the British Army, of whom two were killed and many of the others wounded. One feels that Madame, herself the daughter of a famous soldier, would have been proud of them.

CHAPTER TEN

THE EXHIBITION TODAY

When the First World war ended, John Theodore Tussaud, Madame's great-grandson, was sixty. Of his seven sons, one, Bernard, showed at an early age that he had inherited the talent of his father. While on holiday from school, he would amuse himself by helping his father in the studio, and shortly before the war he was entered as a student at the Slade School. During hostilities he served first in the Gloucesters and then transferred to the Royal Flying Corps, in order to be with his brother Hugh, who was a pilot. Bernard flew as an observer in DH4s and DH9s until the war ended, and after demobilization returned to the Slade School to continue his studies. From 1920 onwards his father began to give him increased responsibility for the modelling, helped by a small highly-skilled staff, of whom the most notable were the artist, Pennichini, and the moulder, George Hopkins. Three of Bernard's aunts, Beatrice, Dolly and Jane Tussaud, assisted with the colouring of the models.

In 1925 Madame Tussaud's was on the point of passing into new hands. A public company had been formed, and on March 18th the Company's prospectus was placed in the hands of the printers. That night, at ten o'clock, people passing along the Marylebone Road saw a red glow coming from the windows. The wiring of an electrically driven organ in the main hall had fused, and within a few minutes the flames had attacked the woodwork. Quickly the fire spread, in spite of the efforts of Messrs. Tussaud's firemen, who were soon joined by the main fire brigade. In a short time the floor of the main upper hall was a glutinous mass of blazing wax. The delicate dresses of queens

and princesses, the silks and satins and kings and courtiers dis-
solved in flame. Iron girders bent like burning matches.
Throbbing hoses snaked up Baron Grant's marble staircase, at
the top of which crouched the sweating firemen, half-choked by
the smoke and stench of burning wax. Above the hiss of the
hoses and the crackle of burning timber rose a roar like a blast
furnace, as flames poured from the upper windows and lit the
sky. From all directions Londoners came running towards the
glare, as the incredible news went round: 'Madame Tussaud's
is on fire!'

The flames quickly ate into the room containing the precious
relics of Napoleon. The great coach which had borne him
through the snows of Russia, his bed from St. Helena, his
Coronation robes, jewels and orders crumbled into white ashes.
Soon the upper floors were completely gutted, and while the
Hall of Tableaux on the ground floor escaped the worst effects
of the fire, water cascaded down from the floor above, drenching
ruffs and doublets, farthingales and periwigs in an indiscrimin-
ate deluge. But the occupants of the Chamber of Horrors got
away with a mere soaking, and among them, fortunately, were
most of Madame Tussaud's own valuable death-masks. On the
following morning, as policemen, firemen, and journalists followed John Tussaud and his sons through the foul-smelling
debris, the faces of Robespierre and Marat, of Charles Peace,
William Palmer and their companions, still stared at them, wet
but triumphant, among the ruins.

It was impossible to assess the damage. Many of the relics,
such as those of Napoleon, were irreplaceable. All that remained of Napoleon's coach was the axle, but the knife of the
guillotine survived. Another survivor was a pet parrot, which,
when it had recovered from the shock, delighted the crowds by
repeating endlessly: 'This is a rotten business. . . .'

One discovery did a little to console the Tussaud family.
Although most of the figures had been destroyed, all the moulds
from which they were made—some going back to the time of

Madame Tussaud—were intact. They had been stored in the lower part of the building, which escaped the worst damage. From these precious moulds John Theodore Tussaud, his son and their staff began remaking the entire collection of figures. By 1927 the building had been repaired and partially rebuilt and three years after the disaster the Exhibition again opened its doors.

Visitors found to their delight that most of the familiar features of the old Exhibition had been retained. All the old favourites were back in their places, together with some new figures; and the popular Chamber of Horrors, as horrible as ever, was now a realistic pseudo-Norman dungeon—underground. In the meantime, a new public company had taken over the project, John T. Tussaud becoming one of the directors.

From 1928 to 1939 it continued to develop along well-tried lines, each year seeing new figures taking the place of older favourites as their popularity or news-value declined. J. Ramsay MacDonald, Anthony Eden and Neville Chamberlain were among the new arrivals who still survive, but many more, after a brief appearance, have gone to the melting-pot. By this time the number of figures had risen to about 500, and quite apart from the delicate matter of public interest, it was, and is, impossible to add new figures without taking off display some of the old. Past celebrities can, however, console themselves with the thought that their moulds are always retained.

The toughest survivors are the criminals. Most of those who joined the Chamber of Horrors in the inter-war years are still there. Henry Armstrong (1922), Henri Landru, the 'French Bluebeard' (1922), Frederick Bywaters and Mrs. Thompson (1923), Patrick Mahon, of the 'Crumbles crime' (1924), and Alfred Rouse, the 'blazing car murderer' (1930). One notes with regret, however, that the writer of the modern Catalogue has lost—or does not permit himself—the lip-smacking gusto of his predecessors. No doubt this is due to the need for conforming to the anaemic standards of modern taste; but, personally, I miss those noble appeals to Providence, that fire-and-brimstone morality which the earlier Catalogue writers injected into their notes. Think how they would have dealt with, say Patrick Mahon, of whom the modern Catalogue briefly states: 'He disposed of the body by boiling portions in a copper. . . .' What an opportunity missed!

Now compare Entry No. 53 in the Catalogue of 1849, Marat. The last sentence is enough: 'This execrable wretch might have added to the number of his victims had not a young heroine name Charlotte Corday, with the spirit of a Judith, determined to rid the world of such a monster; and, having obtained access to him in his bath, she, with a knife, laid the tyrant dead at her feet.' Or No. 75, on James Bloomfield Rush: 'The annals of crime must place the name of Rush at the lowest depth of infamy; he was accused in early life of having set fire to a haystack; of having rescued a man from custody; of having afterwards murdered his Wife, his Mother, his Father-in-Law, and, lastly, Mr. Jermy and his Son, and dangerously wounded Mrs. Jermy and her maid; and of having committed forgeries of the blackest dye. He was executed at Norwich, amidst the deepest execrations of the assembled multitude.'

At the time of the Munich crisis, most of the moulds were evacuated to a safe place in the country. Hitler and Mussolini made their appearance in the galleries, but, unlike the Kaiser in the previous war, neither of these figures was ever attacked. But one curious discovery was made which proves that Black Magic still has its devotees in this country. One morning attendants dusting the effigy of Hitler found a ring of pins stuck round the dictator's heart. The same thing had happened to the figure of the dockers' leader, the Honourable John Burns, over a half a century earlier.

On the night of September 8–9th, 1940, the first night of the blitz on London, one of the heaviest bombs fell on Madame Tussaud's, destroying the cinema and restaurant, and slightly damaging the rest of the building. However, within three months the Exhibition opened again and remained open throughout the remainder of the Second World War. Once again it became a popular rendezvous for the troops of Britain and her Allies. Churchill and the War Cabinet, General de Gaulle, General Eisenhower, Field-Marshals Alexander and Montgomery, Admiral Cunningham, Vice-Admiral Mount-batten and Marshal of the R.A.F. Lord Portal were among the War leaders commemorated in wax.

The Second World War produced a new 'Victoria Crosses' Tableau', which was one of the most effective in the Exhibition. Against a backcloth representing the King pinning on the decoration, a number of war heroes were grouped in natural attitudes, waiting their turn to be presented to His Majesty. Leaning against a table was Wing-Commander Guy Gibson, who personally led the squadron which breached the Mohne and Eder Dams. The biographical note said 'He personally made the initial attack on the Mohne Dam from within a few feet of the water, and then circled the area for 30 minutes drawing flak to allow succeeding aircraft a free run. He then led the re-mainder of the Squadron to the Eder Dam, repeating his tactics to ensure a successful attack. He was later lost on operations.'

On his right sat Lieut-Colonel A. C. Newman, who was in charge of the military element in the St. Nazaire Raid on March 27th–28th, 1942: 'One of the first ashore, he led his men brilliantly against vastly superior enemy forces until the demolition parties had completed their work. . . .' And on the left of the Tableau was Captain B. A. W. Warburton-Lee, the first V.C., of the 1939–1945 War, who was killed when leading 'B' Second Destroyer Flotilla in H.M.S. *Hardy* during the historic attack on Narvik. Other V.C.s represented in the Tableau included submarine commander M. W. Wanklyn, Ser-geant J. P. Keneally of the Irish Guards, Group Captain Cheshire, Lieut.-Colonel C. C. I. Merrit of the South Saskat-chewan Regiment, Naik Nand Singh of the 11th Sikh Regiment, and Private Frank John Partridge of the Australian Military Forces

In 1943 John Theodore Tussaud died at the age of eighty-five; and until the year of his death he continued to maintain a close interest in the Exhibition, though for some time its artistic direction had been in the hands of his son Bernard, who was forty-seven at the time of his father's death.

It is interesting to notice how the Exhibition, now more than 150 years old, has adapted itself continuously to the changing times. That was one of Madame's principles, and it is still faithfully followed by her descendants. In recent years, for instance, the Exhibition has made the fullest use of the newest means of publicity. It has been featured in several films, including *Corridor of Mirrors*: the effigy of Eric Portman, which appeared in the film, was until recently on view in the section of the Exhibition devoted to film and stage celebrities. It has formed the subject of several radio programmes, and more recently has appeared in television. Film, radio and television stars now take their place beside the popular idols of earlier times.

During a visit to the Exhibition I had the pleasure of watching Mr. Bernard Tussaud working on one of the newest figures, the radio and television personality, Richard Dimbleby. While he worked he described how the people to be modelled are chosen, and how the figures are made. Most of the current celebrities, he said, 'choose themselves'. Royalty, Prime Ministers, Cabinet Ministers, Chiefs of Staff, distinguished generals, admirals and air marshals are automatically included. The same applies to film, radio and stage stars, though, as there are more of these and their news-value is usually more fleeting, they have to be selected with great care. Popularity polls, stage and film awards, Press and radio publicity are some of the yardsticks used. In the case of notorious criminals, selection is again almost automatic.

The method of making the models is not very different from that used by Madame Tussaud, though modern techniques, e.g. photography, have been brought into use. After the victim has been selected, Mr. Tussaud interviews him, always trying to set him at his ease in order to catch his most natural expression and pose. Throughout the interview the artist is constantly

154

making notes and sketches. Later one of his two assistants takes about thirty photographs from all angles, while the other notes details of colouring, character of the hair, eyes and complexion. While the impression of the subject is fresh in his mind, Mr. Tussaud hurries back to his studio and with his artists spends many hours at his modelling stand making a rough clay head. The first task is to capture a general impression; it is not until later, with the help of photographs and sketches, that the artist gets down to the long, laborious and often exasperating job of modelling the finished head. This part of the work is pure sculpture. No moulds are made direct from the face, as sometimes occurred in Madame's day, as this method is unsatisfactory, the weight of the wet plaster of Paris distorting the features.

Meanwhile, another member of the staff has obtained from the subject's tailor or dressmaker a complete list of his or her measurements, and from these he makes a body from strengthened plaster of Paris. As the body will be concealed by clothes, wax is only used for modelling the visible parts.

When Mr. Tussaud is satisfied with his portrait, the clay head is ready for moulding. At this point, the moulder, Mr. George Hopkins, or his son, brings his skill to bear on the subject. The finished clay head, now thoroughly dry, is encased in wet plaster of Paris, which is allowed to dry and harden. Obviously the whole head cannot be covered at once, so the mould is made in sections, each section being fitted with a system of plugs and sockets so that when it is reassembled each section will be in correct alignment with its neighbours.

Then the mould is carefully cleaned and assembled, and the sections tied firmly together with cord. Through the open base the moulder pours a mixture of molten beeswax and a small quantity of vegetable wax, which has been previously prepared and coloured so that it exactly matches the basic flesh-colour of the subject. We were shown a number of wax discs, each of a slightly different colour, and labelled with the name of the model for which it was intended.

The hot wax cools from the outside inwards, and when it has

formed a crust of about one and a half inches thickness the surplus wax is poured out, leaving a hollow shell, which is left to harden. Afterwards the artist carefully removes traces of the seams left by the mould-joints, and the head is ready for the next operation—fitting eyes and hair. Eyes are usually a problem. They are surgical glass eyes, carefully chosen to match those of the subject, but placing them in the correct position sometimes takes more than a day's continuous trial and experiment. The ideal is so to set them in the face that they appear to follow the visitor as he walks around the model. The insertion of the hair also requires great skill.

Human hair is used, bought mainly in Italy and Scandinavia; invariably it is female hair, cut from the heads of nuns when they enter a convent. Danny Kaye's beautiful auburn locks may have come from some Titian-haired Italian beauty. To insert the hair, the head is first gently heated until the wax softens, and *each hair is inserted individually* into the wax, a job taking up to two months. Great care is taken to see that the waves and set of the hair are exactly as those of the subject.

Now the head is added to the body, which has been given a coat of paint to seal the plaster and prevent dust working through the clothes. Next the hands are modelled. As it would take too long to model these in the same way as the head, the subject usually visits the studio and a cast of his or her hands is taken in plaster of Paris; then a wax impression is taken from the mould, and with a little finishing the hands are ready to be fitted to the model. All that remains is to dress the figure; usually the subject provides his own clothes. For instance, Marshal Tito, after prolonged negotiation through the Yugoslav Embassy, provided the magnificent uniform which his figure now wears. Her Majesty Queen Juliana of the Netherlands also supplied the magnificent robe worn by her effigy.

Many subjects take particular care to state how their clothes should be worn. The murderer George Haigh, executed in 1949, is an example. When he learned, on the day before his execution, that his figure would appear in the Chamber of

Horrors, he expressed great satisfaction as he sat in the Death Cell. He gave strict instructions as to how his clothes should be worn by his model; trousers with a knife-edge crease, shirt-cuffs one inch below the sleeves, tie carefully pressed and hair immaculate.

All the costumes are brushed and dusted each morning, and periodically dresses are taken away for a more thorough cleaning. Surprisingly, even the clothes on these static models wear out and have to be replaced, sometimes at great cost. The dress worn by Her Majesty Queen Mary, specially made to her own design, cost £500. The clothing for a Court group consisting of seven figures cost well over £1,000. Twenty yards of silk velvet for the figure of King Edward IV cost over £9 a yard. Only the finest fabrics are used, some of them made by specialist firms which have been making royal robes for as long as Madame's has been in existence.

The colouring of the faces, all that now remains to be done, is carried out by a secret method which has been handed down from Madame Tussaud, who learned it in turn from her uncle, Philippe Curtius. When the model finally takes its place in the galleries, it will, if required, last for more than twenty years. In time, however, the wax tends to go yellow, and the hair wears out through constant brushing, combing and shampooing. For this reason, some of the older models in the Exhibition have been re-cast several times from the original moulds. These precious moulds, running into thousands, are the heart of the Exhibition, and though some were destroyed in the blitz of 1940, most still survive.

It is a strange experience to see the fascinating disarray of Mr. Tussaud's studio; half-finished models stand in corners; on the paint-splashed bench is the head of the one of the newest celebrities; on the shelves are older favourites who have come into dock for renovation. On one shelf I noticed, side by side, the heads of the Comte de Lorge, Danny Kaye, the Duke of Gloucester and George Bernard Shaw. Moving about among this happy confusion are the artist and his assistants, white-coated, with clay, wax and plaster on their hands and smocks, surrounded by rows of shelves piled with hundreds of moulds, some of them more than a century old. Each of these moulds carries a number and the name of the person represented. Here is Lord Nelson; there is Charles Peace; and not far away the Duke of Wellington lies cheek by jowl with Napoleon Bonaparte. A thousand years of history lie on these dusty shelves, modelled by the little woman from Strasbourg and the family she founded.

From the studio I wandered into the Exhibition itself, packed with its usual Saturday morning crowd. Many men and women from the provinces were there, recognizable by their football team rosettes; for this was the day of the Cup Final. There were tired mothers with strings of eager children; a few soldiers and airmen on leave, and here and there an obvious foreign visitor, looking slightly puzzled as he glanced from his Catalogue to the staring, pink-cheeked effigies with their delicate ivory hands.

In spite of the modernity of many of the figures, there is still a curiously Victorian atmosphere about Madame Tussaud's. Even the crowds, once they enter the Grand Hall, seem to have left the hurrying, harassed twentieth century. Their voices are hushed as they enter the presence of the great. 'Mingle with the Mighty' says the placard outside, and though they have seen most of these ladies and gentlemen many times in the newspapers and magazines, on the movies or television, still they approach them with strange respect, as if these waxen dolls were somehow nearer to reality than any photograph or moving picture. They stare at the Royal Family, magnificent in their regalia, at Field-Marshal Viscount Montgomery, looking unusually young and pink, at General Eisenhower; and beside him Washington, with his black velvet, lace ruffles and prim, old-maidish face.

How many of these visitors recognize, one wonders, that the effigy of Washington was made by Madame Tussaud while the President was alive; that Eisenhower was made only yesterday?

To them it all seems one. But to us, who have made the long journey which began when Marie Grossholtz came to Paris to join her uncle, there is a special fascination in seeking out the models which she made. Most of them are still there, not separated from the rest, but mingling indiscriminately with those produced only a few years ago.

In a corner of another Hall, next to Lord Macaulay, who stands at the edge of the Literary Group, are the Royal Family of France, Louis XVI and Marie-Antoinette, the little Duchesse d'Angoulême and the Dauphin, just as Marie modelled them in Paris. The Literary Group itself, though it now includes sixteen figures, from Chaucer to Wells, contains two which she modelled with her own hands, Lord Byron and Sir Walter Scott. Beside the Royal Group stands her Voltaire, and even the grotesque Madame Sappé, the 'old coquette who teased her husband's life out', still displays her wrinkled charms.

Descend to the Chamber of Horrors, and among the mean, undistinguished faces of Victorian and Edwardian criminals you will find the death-heads of Marie-Antoinette and Louis XVII, Robespierre and Fouquier-Tinville, Carrier and Hebert, just as she modelled them as they came from the guillotine. The same knife which cut off their heads stands near by. Marat still lies in his bath, and the bearded, emaciated Count de Lorge is the first face we see as we descend the steps to the Chamber.

What is the secret of the appeal of the waxwork figure? That it still exists there is no doubt, nor is it losing its hold. Last year over one million people paid their money to see the famous and the infamous. Why, one asks, do people who have seen Bette Davis and Richard Dimbleby moving on the screen pay to see them static in an Exhibition? Perhaps, after all, there is some anthropomorphic magic in it. In reality or on the cinema screen, which mirrors reality, these people are elusive, mobile; they escape our reach. But here they are motionless. We have got them. Friend and enemy alike, we can walk round and up to them, stare them out of countenance, look at them from un-flattering angles; feel, if not superior, at least that they are made

159

of common clay—like us. Is that the secret which Madame Tussaud understood?

Let us take one last look at her as she stands in the Grand Hall, dwarfed by all the other figures which crowd around her; there she stands at the foot of the 'Sleeping Beauty', the beautiful Madame St. Aramanthe who was 'executed at the command of Robespierre'. Under the lace-trimmed Victorian poke-bonnet, shrewd brown eyes stare at us from behind steel-rimmed spectacles. The lips have a slight downward turn; the chin is firm, the nose strong. A woman of character. A woman who knew what she wanted—and what we wanted—and gave it to us.

But one suspects—and who can blame her—that she did not think much of us.